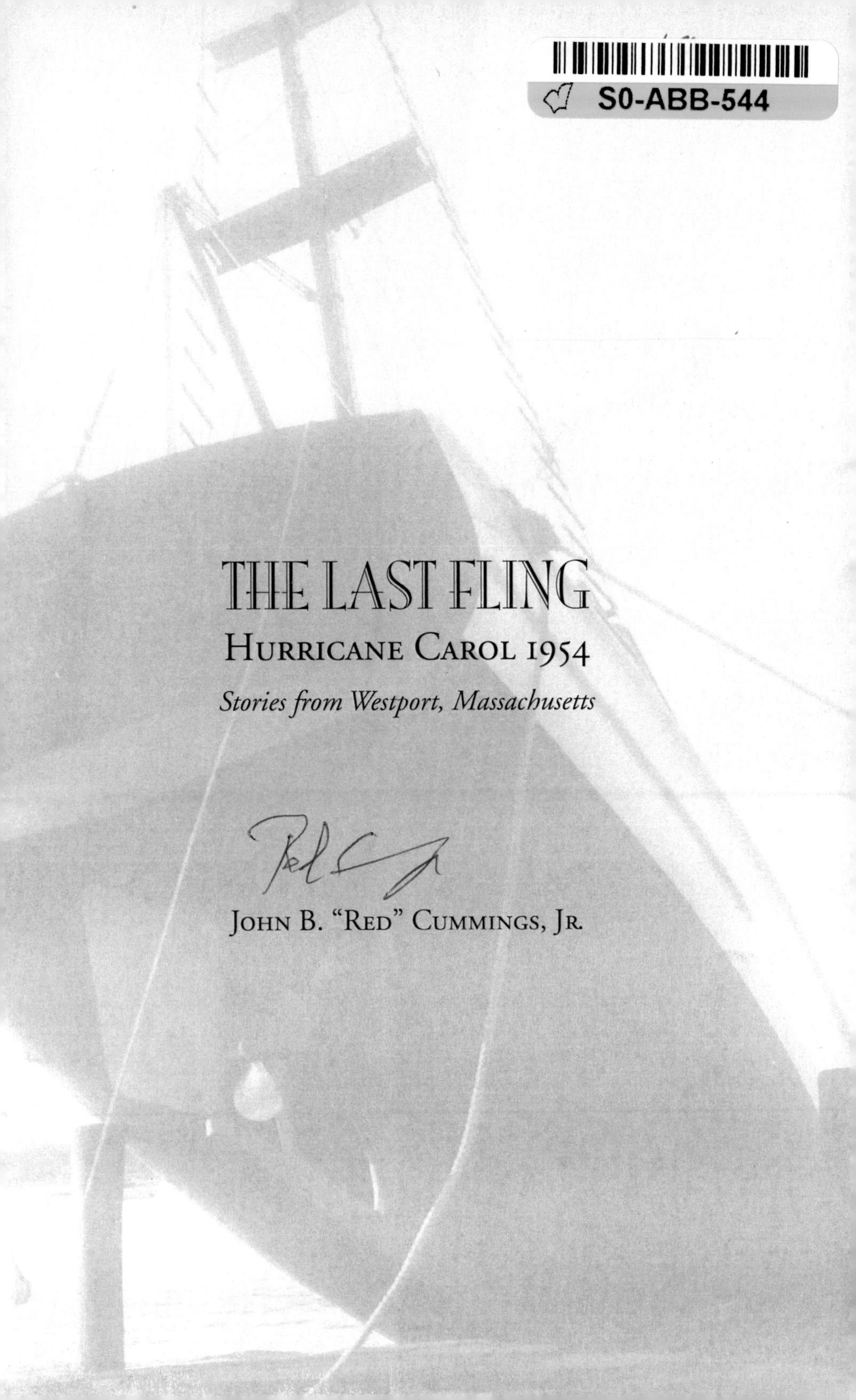

THE LAST FLING

Hurricane Carol 1954

Stories from Westport, Massachusetts

John B. "Red" Cummings, Jr.

All inquiries should be addressed to:

John B. Cummings, Jr.
The Last Fling
46 Hillside Road
Westport, MA 02790
Tel. 508.636.2831
Fax 508.636.6831
or
Info@thelastfling.net

ISBN 978-1-4507-7648-6

Cover Design by David McIlwaine and Mary Senra.

Photo courtesy of The Herald News.

Printed and bound by Senco Printing, Inc. in Fall River, Massachusetts USA.

4 6 8 10 7 5 3

Dedication

To my parents, Angela and John B. who made it possible for me and my family to live in and enjoy Westport for over 58 years in good weather and bad.

And

To my wife, Paula who has provided me with love and affection and positive reinforcement not only during the writing of this book but for more than 30 years.

Preface

The Last Fling evolved from my desire to talk to family, friends and neighbors, and others to come, about what life was like in idyllic Westport, Massachusetts, in the early part of the mid-20th century. The area, Acoaxet in particular, was often dubbed an "exclusive vacation enclave". Yes, it was a vacation spot but for those of us who lived there we never viewed our little slice of heaven as "exclusive," just undiscovered.

While writing about that time in this place, I realized that the amazingly powerful focal point of that period needed to become the primary focus of my effort. Hence: Hurricane Carol.

It was an event that I experienced up close and personally. And it was an event that will happen again despite the absence of such destruction in nearly a half-century. Hurricane Bob touched a part of this generation in 1991 - 20 years ago - but even those now at mid-life have not felt the fury of a Northern Atlantic tropical storm knocking on their door during the summer season. Another will come, that is a promise, and we must be ready to prevent not only the loss of things, but of life. We must learn by experience to survive as nearly all the Westport people that experienced Carol did.

It was my intent to paint a picture of this seaside Massachusetts town prior to the explosion of the technical advances we experience today. It was utopia then, for adults as well as their offspring just as most seaside communities were during that period of our American history. It was pre-Cold War, sunny summer days and cool, ocean breeze evenings. It was the ideal place to spend weeks of summer vacation.

There was never any talk about hurricanes, despite the fact that only ten years previous one had grazed the coastline, and only sixteen years earlier the "Long Island Express" had decimated Westport among other coastal towns. GH38 and Carol were the two great New England hurricanes in the past 100 years and only one had been extensively chronicled. Very few discuss the potential devastation from tornados and floods but 2011 has seen record destruction form these events.

As I researched the written record regarding Carol, I found a dearth of information as it pertained to the Massachusetts coastline. Charles Orloff at Blue Hills Observatory had highlighted the event in eastern Massachusetts in his book. Local newspaper accounts published journals primarily of photos, but I could find nothing that told the various tales of disaster and bravery that could have occurred anywhere, but particularly in Westport, on August 31, 1954.

I had read, and enjoyed, R.A.Scotti's Sudden Sea, Everett Allen's A Wind To Shake The World and Cherrie Burns' Great Hurricane 1938, but I found nothing that told the story of Carol along the southeastern Massachusetts coast in 1954. Perhaps there were not the same dramatic stories to tell, but we had our share as others who have experienced a natural disaster also have, and they are chronicled on the following pages. After everything is said and done, Carol may have been a more vicious cyclone than the one in 1938, but the "Long Island Express" had done all the real dirty work not long before.

There were no warnings for either event, but the former found homes on beaches to destroy and lives to take in the cover of darkness.

Carol arrived in the morning hours, years after only a few foolhardy souls had built new homes on the beaches, and fortunately, very few lives were lost.

My own life had placed me squarely in the story. That terrifying day, I had the opportunity to open the Acoaxet Club clubhouse kitchen door to Jimmy, the Cozy Cab bus driver, after he had marched up the golf course from the safety of his pond boat life raft. His full story had to be gleaned from newspaper articles along with my first hand account since he has long since passed away when I set out on this undertaking. But I found one of his bus passengers was still living in the area: Mary McGowan O'Toole. Her sidekick that day - Dana Plante - had died in military training before the 1950's were over. I did, however, track down and interview his twin brother, Dale, who is now living in sunny Arizona. In 2004 at Westport Point, a fiftieth anniversary survivors' party was held and video interviews were conducted and hurricane stories told but there were no Westport Harbor folk present to relate their adventures. I have tried to combine the most interesting from both sides of the Westport River into this memoir.

As I informed people of my endeavor, more came forth with: "Did you speak to.... he / she has a great story to relate." Survivors came out of the woodwork. Many were interesting and many duplicated other tales I had heard. Some clarified bits of information that over the years were embellished while everyone has their own vivid and not-so-vivid recollection of the events of that day and time. Some, but not all, whose stories are told herein were afforded the opportunity to verify facts before the book went to print. But I found that even within families there was disagreement as to what happened on that day. But as is the universal nature of crisis we all have our own story to tell.

I also subscribe to the saying that a picture is worth a thousand words and to that end this effort is full of photos that I believe add greatly to my factual written word. I think that the photo of *The Last Fling* sitting on the dock best denotes the events of the day. I have tried to capture the time and the place and the forcefulness of Carol in a way that future generations could best relate and leave people in its wake.

Since this effort began as a history for my heirs, longtime friends and new ones who have not lived in Westport until recently, it is they who I hope will take the most pleasure in reading it. I have enjoyed and been educated myself by this writing and if others, outside those for whom it is intended, also find it interesting and /or informative and get pleasure from it, then that is a bonus. Heed the warning; another massive hurricane will come and lay siege to this town and others along the southern New England coast. Be it personal or from nature's fury, let us hope it departs with little destruction in its wake.

I would also like to extend my apologies in advance to anyone whose name is spelled incorrectly or to anyone whose story does not appear as exactly as communicated to me. Thank you for your forbearance.

Foreword

In 1989 at age 64, I thought about the genealogy of my family. The records are there. Beginning in 1610, they show the dates of births, weddings and deaths. But, what did all those people do during their lives? I know very little, so I started writing for future generations to read - not only my own history but that of Westport as well.

John "Red" Cummings in this book, "The Last Fling", has performed a great service for readers interested in the 1954 hurricane. He reports not only on the storm but also on the people who survived and those who did not. The 1954 hurricane was not forecast to hit this area so most people were not ready for that big wind and high sea. It is all here in "The Last Fling".

This book is great reading for anyone but especially for residents of Westport and the surrounding towns. John has done the kind of research that will make the readers feel they know the people and the stresses they suffered during a hurricane. The book will be enjoyed by many future generations who are interested in local history.

Carlton "Cukie" Macomber

Contents

– Part One –

(Chart courtesy of NOAA)

CHAPTER I

Summer Time and the Livin'...

There was a lot going on in the atmosphere along the south coast of Massachusetts during the month of August 1954. Early in the month an all-time record rainfall soaked the city of Fall River and its environs including Westport. In a 24 hour period starting on August 9, 1954 nearly seven inches of rain were recorded. After a generally fair and warm summer the last week of August turned cool and unsettled with frequent late day thunderstorms.

Beginning August 30 an upper level disturbance pulled a tropical storm up the country's eastern seaboard from North Carolina into the Gulf Stream and along the Virginia coast. By 10 o'clock that evening she was strengthening. This was no fish storm - one that remains out over the water never to touch land. A westerly wind current in the jet stream directs storms toward shore, and on this day, the jet stream's movements did just that ...amid a confluence of time and tide that would create a historic hurricane.

I was a boy of 9 the day she hit my summer hometown of Westport, Massachusetts. This is the story of that.

Like all coastal New Englanders on August 30, my parents certainly did not know what was going on in the ocean to the south of Westport. Nor did the fishing boat captain, Ted Hebden, whom they had contacted to arrange an ocean fishing trip with family friends that day. Registered out of Providence, Rhode Island, since Hebden maintained his business there, the swordfish boat with its crow's nest and pulpit sailed out of Westport Point not far from Hebden's West Beach Road home in the section of town known as Horseneck. None of us realized at the time that the name of our chartered fishing boat, *The Last Fling*, would be so prophetic.

Our fellow voyagers for the day were the McDuff family. Doctor Henry Mc Duff, a respected Providence obstetrician and his wife, Charlotte were renting a cottage in Westport Harbor on Acoaxet Road just south of Atlantic Avenue. On the day before the storm made her move up the Atlantic coast and on us, we had joined the McDuffs and their children, Henry, and Charlotte on a sea voyage. None of us were fishermen but a half-day fishing trip out of Westport Point, sounded exciting. Mrs. McDuff was the daughter of one of my Dad's best friends from his days at Harvard, and my father felt personally responsible for her welfare and enjoyment while the family vacationed in Westport Harbor.

The boat and her captain arrived mid-morning in Westport Harbor, at the Charlton family wharf where we boarded. Captain Hebden had replaced his previous boat, the *Bugz*, only a year or so earlier and declared this new vessel to be his last boat purchase. He named her accordingly: *The Last Fling*.

The air was heavy, almost tropical, as we motored down the calm Westport River past the outcropping of rocks known as the Knubble at the mouth of the river into the open ocean. That was the last time I saw water until hours later when the swordfish boat returned to the river. I was not the only person on board down below using the head but it seemed that way. None of us had the benefit of Dramamine. We were like a cork, pitching, bobbing and weaving in Rhode Island Sound for a good portion of the day.

The tip of land that projects into the mouth of the Westport Harbor is referred to as the Knubble on nautical charts but locals call it the Point of Rocks. It is a long stretch of massive outcropping high at the end of a barrier beach between the ocean and river and creates a

17
TOWN OF WESTPORT
MASSACHUSETTS
87
WESTPORT HARBOR
THE AREA WAS FIRST KNOWN AS THE ACOAXET INDIAN PLANTATION. THE APPEARANCE OF AN UNBROKEN SHORELINE LATER CAUSED THE BRITISH TO NAME THE HARBOR "THE DEVIL'S POCKET HOLE". UNABLE TO NAVIGATE THE ENTRANCE IN THE WAR OF 1812, THEY FIRED A CANNON BALL THROUGH THE WALL OF THE DAVIS HOUSE AND RETREATED. MANY A MARINER HAS BEEN HUMBLED TRYING TO NAVIGATE THE ENTRANCE TO THIS PEACEFUL RIVER.
IN THE 19TH AND 20TH CENTURY THE HARBOR BECAME A POPULAR DESTINATION FOR A WEALTHY SUMMER CROWD THAT FILLED THE HOTELS AND COTTAGES, FROLICKED ON THE BEACHES AND DANCED IN THE CASINO. RUM-RUNNING STORIES ABOUND AND CAPTAIN KIDD'S TREASURE MAY STILL EXIST ON LINIKEN ISLAND ACROSS THE CHANNEL.

Town of Westport Historical marker

treacherous entrance for casual sailors attempting a visit to Westport. The shoreline gives an unbroken appearance to the untrained eye from the ocean. A small opening - the river mouth - appears between Horseneck (derived from an Indian word, Hassanegk, meaning: a house made of stone) and the Point of Rocks. It was once called "The Devil's Pocket Hole" by the British who were unable to navigate the entrance to the harbor in the War of 1812.

In 1925, during Prohibition, rumrunners made use of the harbor's secluded shoreline to bring in contraband, according to the 2008 Westport Historical Society publication, Images of America Westport, one brazen rumrunner who was caught and found guilty in a Fall River Court and fined $100 demanded that his lawyer now pay him for the bottle of scotch he had given him. The residents of Westport have always enjoyed a cocktail or two…or more.

Our sword fishing boat bobbed and dipped and rolled for what seemed like an eternity. Some on board cast a line to fish; I did not care, as I just wanted to return to terra firma. Our captain admitted it was unusually rough that day but someone still caught a fish. Neither was of any consolation to me but it did perhaps provide a foreboding of what was coming up the ocean from the south in the next twenty-four hours. What path would she take?

That was the question baffling the folks at the National Weather Bureau in Washington, D.C., as there were no satellites and no weather ships in the Atlantic Ocean due to federal budget cuts in the Dwight D. Eisenhower presidential years. It made predicting the path of hurricanes, already notoriously fickle, nearly impossible. The best they could do and did was issue a warning to ships and "a small craft advisory" for the New England coast.

The living was certainly easy if you were a nine-year-old boy spending his first full summer in Westport Harbor/Acoaxet.

Times were different in 1954. My mother, like most women at that time, smoked and drank alcohol even when she was pregnant with me. Our homes were loaded with lead paint and asbestos. My father drove a car that had no seat belts or air bags. I drank from a garden hose, not from my own private bottle of water and I even shared many a bottle of NuGrape and Orange Crush soda with multiple friends and no one ever got sick. I did not have a Playstation, Nintendo or an X-box. Little League baseball had tryouts and those of us who never made the team joined the other rejects at the park playing stickball. And if I got into trouble at play or at school, I got into more trouble when I got home - I wasn't bailed out.

Someone hitting a golf ball over two hundred fifty yards was a big deal. The Red Sox had not won a World Series since 1918 and getting tickets for the games at Fenway Park was no problem. Fans could even afford to pay for their own tickets and not be dependent upon corporate sponsors to give away a seat. Tennis players wore white and used wooden racquets. The Patriots did not exist and golfers walked courses with caddies and did not ride in carts.

Westport Harbor/Acoaxet and Westport Point/Horseneck are areas of Westport, Massachusetts, in the most southerly part of the state where the Commonwealth of Massachusetts and the State of Rhode Island are kissed by the Atlantic.

The Westport Harbor land mass is in the most southerly section of Westport and is bounded on the south by the ocean, on the west by the town of Little Compton at the Rhode Island state line, on the east by the West Branch of the Westport River and on the north by Adamsville, a hamlet in the town of Little Compton. Originally part of an area then called Seconet, which became Little Compton, the land was annexed to the neighboring town of Dartmouth in 1741 when the Royal Decree changed the boundary lines. The most westerly section of town was first known as Acoaxet Indian Plantation in 1787 and A-Coke-Sit (as it is pronounced) has three meanings according to Wampanoag Indian translations: "a fishing promontory" or a "place of small fields" as well as "land on the other side of little land."

The Point and Horseneck area are bounded on the west by the west branch of the Westport River, on the south by the ocean, the east by the town of Dartmouth and the north by Fall River. The entire town of Westport is fifty square land miles and water encompasses another fourteen and a half miles. It is one of the largest communities (geographically speaking) in the state of Massachusetts. Named Westport because it was the westernmost port in the Massachusetts Bay Colony, at one time in the not too distant past it claimed more cows than people. It sits at fifty feet above sea level but a large section of town along the coast is at sea level and is in the flood plain and velocity zone for storms. Westport is a rural community founded on whaling, farming and fishing - the latter two remain active to this day. While the Westport Point/Horseneck section of town was centered more on water- related activities, Westport Harbor was an idyllic place to enjoy the bathing beach at Elephant Rock, the Charlton Wharf area with the still waters of the sandy riverfront beach at the mouth of the Westport River, and the Acoaxet Club with golf, tennis, and a clubhouse with dining facilities and a few guest rooms for overnight visitors.

In his prospectus for the development of Goosewing Beach on the Westport Harbor/Little Compton town lines, acclaimed Fall River surgeon Philemon E. Truesdale wrote in his foreword in 1934: "Those who come to this district will have as an incentive not only bathing, boating, the cool breezes and golf but sensitive and loving eyes for the natural phenomena which here rank so high among the wonders of New England."

Early Westport, ca. 1900 prominent people from Fall River, Massachusetts, many of whom were successful in the cotton business at that time, developed the Westport Harbor/Acoaxet section of Westport at the turn of the twentieth century while other professional

(Postcard courtesy of the Albert E. Lees Jr. collection)

and business folks from New Bedford settled in Horseneck and East Beach areas. Fishermen settled in the Point area.

A century ago a day trip to the ocean was still a significant undertaking by horse and carriage as it is approximately twenty miles from Fall River to Acoaxet and a similar distance from New Bedford to the Point. Visitors to the Harbor often stayed at the Sowle Hotel along the riverside at the mouth of the harbor. (The hotel later became part of Macomber Brothers enterprises known as the Harbor Inn/Ogden's Store). Other vacationers to Acoaxet enjoyed the views from the highest point in the area at the Howland House on the opposite side of the peninsular from the river. The structure, privately owned, still stands on the rise of land that dominates the horizon. Locals called one, "the inn" and the other, "the hotel", but they were both essentially bed and breakfast establishments. More inns and hotels lined the rocky shoreline at East Beach enjoying unobstructed ocean views. The Surfside Hotel with sixteen rooms, the Ocean

(Howland House photo courtesy of Westport Historical Society)

House and Kingfisher House, which also sold staples and snacks like Ogden's, were popular overnight accommodations for visitors.

As time passed, many early 20th century visitors bought land and constructed their own grand cottages on or near the waterfront. Those erected on Elephant Rock Beach, East Beach or in the dunes on Horseneck were built in Queen Anne or shingle style with a deep veranda. Many boasted round, whimsical turrets. Some were also constructed with beach rock that may have looked formidable but provided little or no protection when hurricanes hit.

As the Harbor and Acoaxet area was being developed, the local residents saw the need for a country club "for the purpose of establishing and maintaining places for social meetings," according to the 1919 Club charter, "encouraging athletic exercises, yachting and healthful recreation and providing proper means and places thereof.... in general, promoting the civic improvement of that part of the town of Westport, in said Commonwealth, commonly known as Westport Harbor or Acoaxet and the welfare and enjoyment of the people who dwell therein." Acoaxet was and still is the tax revenue "cash cow" for the town since the area has few town services and because it is principally a summer colony with very few children attending the town schools.

By 1954, getting to and from the Harbor and the Point by automobile was no longer an all-day event and even "those Providence people," as I remember they were called, could make the trip easily. Not so for Bostonians until President Eisenhower proposed the interstate highway system and route 24 between the Boston suburbs and Fall River was constructed. Television became more commonplace but it still took five minutes for it to warm up and the need for a roof top antenna for decent reception was another expense that most summer homes did not incur. TV had gone to the dogs with Lassie and Adventures of Rin Tin Tin being two of the top programs and Smokey the Bear warning viewers "only you can prevent forest fires." The Lone Ranger and the singing cowboy, Gene Autry, along with Roy Rogers and his wife, Dale Evans, with their horses, Trigger and Buttermilk, dominated the Saturday morning schedule of must-see television shows. My parents selected the shows that we would watch such as Howdy Doody with Uncle Bob's Peanut Gallery, Jack Benny and "The Honeymooners" with Jackie Gleason. There were no cable television or satellite dishes and only two channels were all summer residents could view back then. Radio was still the primary communication vehicle at the time.

A postage stamp for first class mail was three cents and rock and roll was just born. Vaccinations and booster shots for children were the rage and a tonsillectomy was the era's most popular medical procedure. Those medical advances gave birth to the Doctor and Nurse Bags with toy stethoscopes and syringes – every kid had to have one.

Shortly thereafter, Disney saw the value of a rodent and Mickey and Minnie Mouse items became the rage among children.

Hardly anyone's mom worked outside the home and a quarter was a decent allowance for a kid. You could buy a pack of baseball cards - that turned out to be valuable years later if your mother had not thrown them out - with that awful pink slab of bubble gum for five pennies. And what would the day have been like without eating (yes, eating) packets of Kool-Aid? Decisions were made by going "eeny-meeeny-miney-moe" with friends at play and calling out "oly-oly-in-free" made perfect sense to halt a game of Capture the Flag or Kick the Can. Some of us attended a camp run by Bob Wheeler and Harry Pelton two afternoons per week in Steve Howland's old, big barn. We played those games, heard ghost stories and traveled to the riverside beach in an old car with a rumble seat.

But the era was not without worry either. The Russians had built "the bomb," we were told, and that presented the possibility of an atomic attack. Practicing for that dreadful day was commonplace in schools. The Holy Union of the Sacred Heart nuns at the Sacred Heart Elementary School in Fall River instructed the students to hide under desks if the siren went off, because it might be the real thing. In the meantime, youngsters were urged to say the rosary for peace on a daily basis. We were living in peace but simultaneously in fear. But for most children, War was a card game and the ultimate weapon was a water balloon.

In the Harbor in 1954, seventy-nine–year-old Steve Howland had begun to divest himself of his land and buildings. Although he continued to operate the hotel to some degree, he had sold his family farmhouse on Howland Road, and subdivided the land into 65 house lots. (Some people with foresight bought multiple adjacent lots: my father, Jud Hindley, and after Hurricane Carol, Doctor Daniel Gallery, to name a few.)

After selling the large family farmhouse, Howland moved into a small cottage north and adjacent to his hotel where he could still survey the pond, river, ocean and beaches while overseeing his dairy business. His milk processing equipment was in the garage next door and his chicken coop with the vociferous, early-to-rise rooster was next to that. Howland convinced long-term employee, Bud Davis, and his wife, Mary, to move in with him to care for him while still employing Manny Medeiros from nearby Lake Road in Tiverton, Rhode Island, as a farm hand.

Steve maintained a dairy farm for years and would bring in cows from time to time to replenish his small herd of six. The land baron cut and bailed hay from his fields and continued to own two homes on the ocean that he rented out in the summer. The farmer produced, sold, and delivered by automobile non-pasteurized milk and cream, eggs, and veggies. The cream was especially thick and was a treat in coffee or on top of berries. He would add some coffee to his milk and sold coffee milk for five cents a bottle. Many summer residents including my parents refused to drink his milk or eat cream because it was not pasteurized and it was rumored that non-pasteurized milk caused tuberculosis.* Howland held the last raw milk-processing license in Massachusetts.

Steve Howland rented his bathhouses to day-trippers from Fall River as changing and storage rooms and there was access to the beach from the large parking area. Steve's niece, Mildred Foster, owned another set of bathhouses across the road from his to the west. Mildred and her husband, Stuart, also operated a small snack bar for their members and others who wanted a hot dog or burger, a cold drink or ice cream.

* There were no reports that anyone in Westport who ever drank his milk was ever stricken with tuberculosis.

The Foster family allowed local kids to cook and serve from the snack bar never considering the need for Board of Health approval or food handler permits. And no one got sick! The Foster Snack Bar was nothing on the scale of those on Horseneck Beach called Midway and Spindrift. They provided beach access and daily parking for day tripping beachgoers while Foster catered to seasonal bathhouse renters and local residents.

Was it possible for all these businesses, located so close to the ocean, to be spared from the wind and raging surf of a tropical cyclone on approach, steadily, from the south?

Westport and Acoaxet, in particular, had never been a vacation "hot spot" - no nightlife to speak of or movie theaters within fifteen miles. There were drive-in movie theaters in North Westport and North Dartmouth, Massachusetts and Tiverton, Rhode Island, but nothing in close proximity.

The drive-in cost one dollar twenty-five cents per carload including all the kids that could sneak in, stuffed in the trunk. On the night before the hurricane you could see a young Elizabeth Taylor in *Elephant Walk*. If you owned a new Nash automobile for $1,550 at the time, you could go in style to the drive-in. It was important to find a good spot in the parking lot so the car was not stuck behind a pick-up truck. Before turning off the engine a speaker check was vital to assure that the audio into the car from the window speaker worked properly. It was also crucial to be near the concession stand and rest rooms. Movie watchers would return to their vehicles just in time for the first of two feature films armed with multiple treats like popcorn, candy apples, cotton candy and a soda, all for three bucks.

Another entertainment option for Westporters was Lincoln Park, an amusement park in the northeast section of town, on the town of Dartmouth line, where you could enjoy the rides and amusements all day for five cents or meet famous celebrities "in person" like cowboy, Gabby Hayes. The park offered something for everyone: amusements and rides, bowling alleys, a roller rink, concession stands, a picnic pavilion that served delicious clambakes along with a Million Dollar Ballroom for dancing and shows highlighting popular singers. There was also a Tap Room to help quench the thirst of adult visitors. It was a gateway to disease due to all the outings that were held and sick children confined to small spaces. Many parents dictated that it was verboten in the middle of the 1950's when the polio epidemic hit. It was also the site of one of the only two deaths attributed to Hurricane Carol in Westport in '54. The Park finally shut its doors in 1988 but the skeleton of the roller coaster can still be seen when driving along Route 6 in Westport at the Dartmouth town line.

If you went to Fall River to the Durfee Theater on North Main Street with its long entrance hall lined with color and black and white posters heralding coming attractions, chandeliers, and goldfish pond in the lobby, moviegoers could watch Jimmy Stewart in Alfred Hitchcock's thriller Rear Window with Grace Kelly. The movie was a bargain at twenty-five cents and also included at no extra charge were the Looney Tunes and Movie Tone News as well as another full-length feature film. Popcorn was a dime or you could purchase a nickel candy bar to munch on. A chow mein sandwich and a coke for thirty-five cents next door at the China Royal Restaurant followed a night at the movies.

Cocktail parties were followed by dinner dances at the Acoaxet Club in the early 50's. These were always been a popular activity for local adults and teens alike. At that time dinner/dances occurred nearly every other Saturday night and featured eight-piece dance bands like the Ralph Stuart Orchestra or the Ed Drew Orchestra. Both were well known in society circuits playing at galas in Newport, Rhode Island, and Palm Beach, Florida. The bands were far too large for the Acoaxet Club dining room and rocked the neighborhood as well as the clubhouse. The club dances were not formal but tie and jackets were required even for teens. (Bermuda shorts and knee socks were not only acceptable but in vogue.) Club "jack-of-all-trades" Ed Phinney strictly enforced a dress code at the door. By the end of the night the ties and jackets had been removed after dancing to the Muskrat Ramble and other swing tunes of the times. Rock and Roll had just been introduced by Bill Haley and the Comets and "Shake, Rattle and Roll" was one of the most popular 45 rpm records at the time, but these exciting new sounds were definitely not included in the dance bands' repertoires.

In 1954, the Acoaxet Clubhouse did not have a full liquor license so members and their guest brought their own bottles of liquor, checked the bottle with the bartender at the bar and were given a numbered ticket. The club provided the set-ups for a nominal fee. Beer and wine were not as popular then as they are today, despite the fact that you could buy a 32 ounce bottle of Budweiser, which could fill "five full glasses" as the ads proclaimed, for only fifty cents. Hard liquor like bourbon and scotch were more the *drinks du jour.*

While there was no minimum age restriction for who could attend a dance, teenagers were always in abundance. Teens could not bring liquor into the clubhouse or buy beer and wine, but they often memorized, and then recited, a member's liquor ticket number to a busy bartender who would fill it up and then add the requested mix. "Bottle thirty-one with ginger ale, please." By the end of a dance night, the members who had loosened their ties both literally and figuratively, had no idea of how much liquor they consumed from their individual bottles and at midnight when the bands were scheduled to stop playing, they passed the hat. Not knowing when to quit, the revelers still in attendance generated adequate funds to keep the band playing for another hour or so, much to the dismay of the neighbors not in attendance.

One neighbor living north of the clubhouse and literally downwind of the area's prevailing southwest winds was a member of the club's Board of Governors. A prominent Boston bank executive and not one to dance the night away, he proposed at a board meeting that the use of an alarm clock was the best way to control the situation. "Set the clock for midnight and when the alarm rings, that is the end of the music," he pleaded. The idea was discussed, but ultimately, the bands played on. It is unknown if there was any connection, but the Labor Day dance in 1953 was shut down after midnight by the Westport Police after an anonymous complaint was received.

CHAPTER 2

Kids Stuff

My father and mother, and before they were a couple, my father alone, spent a great deal of time in Westport Harbor. He was an original shareholder of the Acoaxet Club. His brother and family rented Doctor Ralph W. French's house on Elephant Rock beach where my Dad enjoyed frequent visits until it was swept away in the 1938 hurricane. French was the son of Enoch French who benefited from the Industrial Revolution and was well known in the cotton textile industry in the area. Doctor French was also one of ten founding members of the Acoaxet Club and a prominent surgeon at the Truesdale Hospital in Fall River. Not only did his primary residence on the beach get destroyed in the '38 hurricane, but his boathouse on the river was also washed away. He, like others at the time, experienced a double hit and very few properties in those days were insured. The one house in the Acoaxet area on Atlantic Avenue, which was insured, sustained no damage.

Thirty-six years later, the same fate would befall another noted Fall River surgeon whose home was about 200 yards to the west on the same beach. The only thing left of the French house was the stairs where my parents and I often picnicked. Later as a teenager I often partied at the five remaining concrete steps with friends as my heirs have done and continue to do so. At some point after a strong coastal storm over the last 55 years, the steps split into two sections. Two more steps are buried in the sand in the vicinity of the others like Captain Bly's buried treasure. *

*During the writing of this book, the first and only hurricane, Bill, to reach New England on August 22, 2009 sideswiped Westport. Although there was little wind or rain - he was well east of Nantucket and posed no danger to the coast - the surf was worth viewing as it crashed over Elephant Rock. High tide produced significant beach erosion and a section of the missing steps rose again out of the sand like a phoenix. More winter storms submerged the remaining stairs into the sand with only a periscope–like top now visible. The next storm whatever time of year it may arrive may uncover them totally. And it did! On September 3, 2010, Hurricane Earl unearthed the two remaining two steps.

In 1936, my father, John B. Cummings, married my mother, Angela King. They experienced the 1938 and 1944 hurricanes together but not in Westport. In 1954, all three of us would witness the power of the wind and ocean from the closest vantage - point.

With the exception of an occasional overnight at the Acoaxet Club, our time as a family in the early 50's was spent at Elephant Rock Beach during the day or on the Westport riverside. Occasionally, we

Dr. French's steps to his oceanfront home after GH38
(Photo courtesy of Anne Tripp Hopkins)

trekked to docks at Westport Point for an early evening picnic, an area that would be totally flooded during major coastal storms. We often climbed onto the Point of Rocks, for picnics as well. The menu for those evening excursions included hot tea with lemon and sugar for my parents and cold milk (we had milk at every meal, not water or soda) for my cousin, King Cruger, and me.

The beverages were stored in two glass-lined thermos bottles with hot/cold cups for drinking. King, who was four years older than me, often accompanied us since he, like me, was an only child.

The author (l) and his cousin, King.
(Photo courtesy of J. King Cruger)

"The thermos bottles were lined with mirrored glass and were extremely fragile. I can remember more than once hearing a tinkling noise and hoping we were not going to be drinking out of that bottle," King recalled vividly years later. My parents would enjoy lobster salad sandwiches while King and I partook of peanut butter and jelly on white-no crusts for me, thank you.

On those overnight visits to the Acoaxet Club, my parents enjoyed the view overlooking what is now called Cockeast Pond, also known as Davol's Pond but first called Cockeset Pond. (The Indian name for the area was Coxet and therefore, the original name of the pond was Cockeset.) From the club dining room members and guests looked out to the Westport River with its armada of fishing and sailboats moored in the harbor. They saw the sand dunes at Horseneck Beach or looked over the Atlantic to the Elizabeth Islands. On an exceptionally clear day, they could see the white cliffs at Gay Head on Martha's Vineyard. While they enjoyed dinner and the "million-dollar" view, I was under the watchful eye of my babysitter, young Susan Phinney. Sue was the daughter of the Acoaxet Club golf professional, greens keeper and master of all trades, Ed, and his wife, Ethel.

To kill time with her charge she often took me, accompanied by her mom to the beach. At that time, as it is today, walking the beach attempting to find and collect sand dollars or flat rocks for skipping was great fun for a kid. Back then one could even find mussels and snails in the vernal pools on the beach.

Sand dollars were more common on the beach in the 50's than they are today. They were very fragile, easily broken by the touch and a real treasure if you were lucky enough to find one and bring it home in one piece. They are rarely discovered on the Westport beaches any longer.

Flat rock tossing into the ocean was also a challenge - it was always easier to achieve mastery on the mostly flat river surface. First, the thrower needed to find the perfect rock on the shore. Then the toss (snap of the wrist) determined your result - one skip or less was a failure, two skips got a "no big deal" and five earned a "well done."

Exploring around Charlton's wharf on the riverside was always an adventure. A large rock outcropping into the river next to the wharf afforded ample opportunity for crabbing plus spotting an occasional eel as well as schools of fish. One could join legitimate fishermen from other sections of town and drop a fishing line off the wharf and hope for the best. The best never arrived. As a result of that and our pre-hurricane fishing excursion I have never had any interest in the sport.

The little cottage my parents first rented and then purchased in early 1954 was ideally located near the beach and within walking and biking distance to the Acoaxet Club and Howland Farm.

That summer when I was not riding my bright red Schwinn Corvette bike I spent time trapping grasshoppers in a glass bottle, catching butterflies in a net or chasing fireflies. The highlight of the afternoon was going to watch the six cows being milked by hand by Bud and Manny at Howland's farm, which was a short walk up the road from my house. Kids could help the farmhands pick up the garbage and trash, and create haystacks and load the rectangular bails of hay onto the all-purpose dump truck. They would be unloaded at the barn and hauled up the rickety ladder stairs to the second floor storage area. The small herd would enjoy the cut grass during the cold winter months.

In the summer of 1954, the Howland farm was just the right size for pre-teens kids to enjoy. Cows grazed in fields and drank water from an old bathtub on the west side of Howland Road and then were herded back to the barn for milking by Bud and Manny around four o'clock in the afternoon. Bud and Manny would take over and squirt raw milk at the wide-eyed children watching and the cows would assist by spraying when nature called. Beside the small herd of milking cows there was either a calf or a bull in residence along with feral cats that would survive on mice, rats and cow milk. Turtles and frogs would serenade nightly in the adjacent pond while the small body of water was alit with fireflies. The adjacent large garage stored the tractor and a dump truck that was primarily used for trash pick up.

Bud and friends ride the tractor next to the author's home.
(Photo courtesy of Lorna Phan and Holly Bronhard from Dr. Tony D'Angelo collection)

Trash was collected twice weekly and garbage from in-ground receptacles next to the front doors of the cottages, all without the benefit of gloves. At that time open-air burning of trash was legal and the smell of trash permeated the area frequently. The Howland trash pick-up was limited to the west side of the Harbor and Cockeast Pond. The Meader family did the pick up on the east side.

Kids did not ride on the Meader trucks but there were always youngsters, usually boys, helping with the Howland pick-ups and riding right in the middle of the trash heap in the back of the dump truck - all with parental permission.

In the summer of 1954 Westport Harbor was an idyllic place to grow up. So ideal, in fact, that generation after generation would return with their children each summer to relive their own youth. The

Howland Farm is gone, so is the Bojuma Farm, which was less than two miles away to the north.

Bojuma (so named after the three Tripp children by their father, Phillip: Borden, Judy and Mary) was much larger than Howland's and run by Borden Tripp. When Phillip Tripp purchased the 57-acre farm along River and Cross Roads in 1918 for $8,000 it also included furnishings and fixtures for both the farmhouse and barns. (A motor boat and tender as well as a 1916 Ford Truck and all the vegetables and eggs were included.) Phillip's son, Borden, expanded the farm in 1939 when he bought more land on Cross Road adjacent to the original acreage. It provided summer employment for many a local teen for years. There were as many as 12 people who worked on the farm herding cattle and milking and feeding 160 cows. There were 85 sheep and 100 laying hens and thousands of chickens and turkeys. Milk processing was done in Fall River at the bottling plant, which was overseen by Borden Tripp's wife, Alice, and that facility employed 7 and supplied pasteurized milk to the Westport Schools.

Alice, like Borden, grew up in Westport Harbor. They dated and married in 1929 soon after Bordie graduated from Harvard. Her family, the Dennett's, owned a substantial cottage on Atlantic Avenue that was split in half in the Great Hurricane of 1938. On the following day, the second floor of the house was found three quarters of a mile north with their dog, a dachshund, asleep in fine condition on a bed. As an advertising executive in New York during the Depression, Bordie's first career turned sour, according to his daughter Anne Tripp Hopkins. He and Alice elected to return to Westport and operate his father's farm despite knowing nothing about farming except that he had been brought up on one. They had expected to live on the oceanfront in the home his in-laws were giving them, but that was the one split in half by the hurricane of '38. Bordie, always laid back, was quoted as saying to friends years later, "Well, easy come, easy go."

What he did know was that he loved animals. He oversaw hundreds of acres and two large barns. His cows grazed in fields off River and Cross Roads about one mile inland. He leased other farmland on Brayton Point Road and in an area now known as Pequaw-Honk. His cows were herded first over dirt roads and then asphalt - paved roads back and forth to fields' miles apart. By the late 1940's labor was getting more difficult to recruit for such physically demanding work and Borden could see the handwriting on the wall. In 1954, Borden Tripp also operated Abraham Manchester's General Store in Adamsville, Rhode Island, a few miles north of Westport Harbor. That store was the successor to the Philip Manchester and Son store that operated in the 1800s. After Phillip died, Ab, who lived on the second floor, took over the reins and ran the store until he passed in the late 1940's.

Relatives, Borden and Alice Tripp, couldn't stand the thought of the family store closing, so as farming was becoming more difficult, they saw retail as a possible avenue for escape. They operated the store for over a decade with its famous, much sought after, nine-month aged, Adamsville cheddar cheese. They simultaneously ran the farm. The store provided everything and more on a larger scale than Ogden's in the Harbor. With the advent of a larger Lees Market in Central Village the general store closed but eventually reopened as Manchester's Restaurant and Tavern which was a popular eating and watering hole until around the turn of this century when it burnt to the ground. Bordie held on to the farm through a number of economic ups and downs and major hurricanes including Carol and Edna and Donna until 1964 when he stopped working the farm to become a financial adviser at a local stock brokerage firm. It is still a farm today but not a dairy farm and much of the Bojuma land is now occupied by family homes overlooking the West Branch of the Westport River.

While there was and still is, lots for kids to do, parents still refer to the vacation time in Westport Harbor as going to "Camp Acoaxet". Adults enjoy similar activities: swimming, body surfing, wind surfing, fishing, sailing, golf, tennis, water skiing and social functions. Since the Westport Harbor population is small, there has never been a restaurant within four miles except the food service offered to members of the Acoaxet Club. For a time, the Wib Smith family operated the Spindle Rock Restaurant for lunches and clambakes, but it did not survive. Chowder and clam cakes were the lunchtime special along with a coffee or vanilla cabinet (frappe, if you prefer). After the restaurant closed its doors, the community eventually purchased the property for a yacht club that presently operates at that location on River Road just north of an inlet between the river and Cockeast Pond known as the herring run. The Spindle Rock Club, unlike the Westport Yacht Club further up river in the heart of the harbor, was not operating during Hurricane Carol. It was still a clambake pavilion and lunchtime restaurant operated by Mrs. Smith.

The Spindle Rock Club was not the first yacht club in Westport Harbor. Prior to the 1938 hurricane there was a building located at the base of the Point of Rocks on the riverside where water-based activities were centralized. It was known then as the Westport Harbor Yachting Association and children and adults alike competed for the Charlton Cup just as they did and still do in golf at the Acoaxet Club. The buildings were swept away in 1938 and nothing replaced it in Westport Harbor until the Spindle Rock Club, which sits today in a more protected but still very vulnerable part of the harbor.

1954 was just a typical summer in Westport. An ocean swim followed by a sailing race at Westport Yacht Club either on the river for novices or in the ocean for more advanced sailors or on Cockeast Pond for beginners. Candy and ice cream were purchased at Mrs.

Ogden's store in the Harbor or Lees Market at the Point. A burger or frankfurter and NuGrape were available at Midway or Spindrift at Horseneck or Foster's snack bar. Afternoon tennis or golf at Acoaxet was followed by 4 p.m. milking at the Howland farm cow barn - watch where you step! Finally, it was home for dinner after being off all day. No one ever reported in (no cell phones or texting, how did we all do without it?). Some evenings, we quickly headed back out for a picnic on Gull Rock (before the birds took it over) in the middle of the 99 acre Cockeast Pond. Today, 55 years after Hurricane Carol deposited salt water from both the ocean and river into it; the size of Cockkeast Pond has been reduced by at least 25 percent of its pre-hurricane dimension by the invasive phragmite plant. As the plant takes over the pond, it not only reduces the range for recreational purposes, it also blocks water views, thus reducing the value of adjacent real estate.

Dinner was usually followed by a visit next door to Mrs. Sturtevant's "Dog House" for either a sing-a-long or a game of canasta with other area kids and Mrs. S. "She was our music teacher and we sang almost every night at her cottage with a piano and her golden spaniel", recounted Dail Rhee, nearly 60 years later. Rhee was a teenage neighbor who lived on the oceanfront in 1954. Mrs. Sturdevant rented her main house to a Doctor King and resided in the small adjacent guesthouse, which had a sleeping loft that was only accessible by a wooden ladder. There was a tiny kitchen with a small two-burner propane gas stove and a small refrigerator. The bathroom was nothing more than a toilet and sink. An outdoor shower serviced both homes. The small living area was complete with a couch, a piano, fireplace and folding card table.

When darkness came everyone headed home. There were – and still are - no streetlights in any part of town then to beckon us. It did not take much to tumble off to bed listening to the chirping mating call of the male crickets as they rubbed their back legs together. Fireflies danced outside the bedroom windows warning potential pred-

The "Dog House" and nearby water tower pre-Carol.
(Photo courtesy of Nancy Stropp Marion)

ators that they tasted bad so "stay away" and often provided the light show for the musical crickets. Catching them could happily occupy an entire evening. No television, no computers, no texting or e-mails. Just exhaustion and anticipation for what tomorrow would bring.

They were tranquil times, but soon to be interrupted with historic force.

CHAPTER 3

The Rocks

In the 50's, Elephant Rock Beach Club in the Harbor never closed. There was generally only one life guard on staff with a weekend relief person who took the water temperature in the morning, worked on his sun tan during the day, and departed around 4 p.m. Everyone was then left alone to fend for themselves.

Enter David Morse

A short, blond-haired, muscular, teenage daredevil, Morse challenged the ocean and the rock that resembles an elephant with his inflatable rubber mattress and lack of common sense. He was one of two children of Ken and Helen Morse who lived on River Road about a mile and a half from the beach across the road from Bojuma Farm.

Morse gave his parents fits. If the surf was up, Morse was on top of it, in it and under it. On one occasion he projected his inflatable mattress with his body attached to it off the head of the rock, only to be thrown back against it like a boomerang. Luckily, he was able to paddle back to the beach bloodied and bruised but with not much sympathy from the spectators. If permitted, he would have challenged the surf generated by Carol's fury. But he did not. At least he was not known to have done so. It was rumored that he alone maneuvered the lifeguard chair out to Elephant Rock and set it ablaze. The chair still find its way each summer to the head of the Elephant, but thankfully, without flames.

The Elephant Rock Beach Club Pavilion, as it was called then, had an office with a clerk who signed in members and guests and administered basic first aid; the staff provided access to your bathhouse. Invariably, the lock was rusted, the key would not turn and a shot of oil was needed to gain access. On the weekend there was a Westport auxiliary police officer on duty to help park cars in the lot. Dana Reed also escorted elderly members across the road.

It was spartan but welcoming. A covered sitting area allowed members to escape the rays of the sun and enjoy the view of the ocean. Cold-water showers rinsed the salt water from your body and sand from your feet before heading to a changing locker. Baker and Earle's' bathing club at Horseneck, Westport Yacht Club, Howland's and Foster's in the Harbor provided the same amenities to their members, most of whom were day-trippers from Fall River rather than summer residents of the area.

Most members had lockers; very few came or left in a bathing suit. They left their wet bathing suits, bathing caps and towels in their lockers to dry, but those items were always damp at best, wet at worse, regardless of when you returned.

Hair was so important to the 50's look that no woman wanted to get it wet when swimming, so lavish bathing caps covered in flower petals and rubber spikes became essential beach accessories. Members left beach chairs and more importantly, nail polish remover or kerosene, and cotton balls, in their lockers. When you arrived at the beach for a swim you never knew what you would encounter: a section of beach covered in tar, seaweed, jellyfish, or the dreaded Portuguese man-of-war.

Thankfully, tar has generally disappeared. In 1954, oil tankers that traveled the shipping lanes offshore in front of the beaches of Westport either deposited spills or discharges and tar would end up in the water and all over the beach. It never prevented anyone from taking a dip in the water but it certainly made a mess. Nail polish remover or kerosene and cotton balls to administer the remover usually cleaned up your feet and toes to the extent that allowed you to get home and really work on them.

The jellyfish and Portuguese-man-of-war, also known as "The Bluebottle", is not a single animal but four kinds that attach to each other for survival and are dangerous to humans if stung. The tentacles can reach out one hundred sixty-five feet to sting their prey. The sharp pain can last from minutes to hours. The affected area has a red line with small white lesions. Even a dead specimen on the beach can still sting if touched. They are not always visible in the water so if they are known to be present it is best not to venture out. The sea creatures were ubiquitous in August '54 as the southern Atlantic water made its way north to warm the colder ocean waters around Westport.

The approximately 80-locker Elephant Rock Beach Club structure was built with inexpensive wood that had its pros and cons - knotholes and splinters. If a kid chose to run in the aisles or on the porch – what kid did not? – a splinter was assured. The first manager, backup life guard, Janet Branch Rattray, performed the surgical removal and then treated the victim with stinging iodine that served as a painful reminder to stop running. Iodine was not the only remedy administered to open wounds to prevent infection back then. Mercurochrome was also used but after many years was proved to be dangerous. It is no longer available, but Janet applied it liberally for years. Tincture of Merthiolate was another option, which also is no longer applied to cuts.

The knotholes in the wood served a different purpose. They reduced the privacy in each locker to the kindness of neighbors or the age of the kids next door. Most lockers had three abutters and depending on how bathing suits or towels were hung on the interior pegs dictated the views from the "peepholes". You could outfit your locker any way you pleased but nail polish, cotton balls, a mirror and comb, and baby powder were standard fare along with towels, suits, and bathing caps. Some families stored beach chairs but most visits to the beach were for a swim and not for sun bathing so a chair was an unnecessary luxury for most members. Sit on a wet towel, head into the surf, walk the beach to dry off while looking for sand dollars or flat rocks to skip and then go home. That was the drill.

The configuration of the Pavilion also provided a great nightly hang-out for children. Kids ran and jumped onto the roof of the lockers from row to row while others raced bikes up and down and sometimes off the steps onto the sand below until Mrs. Snow, who lived across the road on Atlantic Avenue, could stand it no longer and started yelling. Some nights when her patience was especially thin she even showed up in person. "You kids don't belong here. Get out before I call the police. Move it. Now!" boomed Flossie. She was very intimidating and, if truth were known, we were more "ascared" of Flossie than we were the cops and we generally obeyed… for an hour or so.

While Newport, Rhode Island, attracted the super wealthy from all over the world and the Sakonett section in Little Compton, Rhode Island, was home to the successful Providence professional, Westport was the place where the post–cotton-generation from Fall River and New Bedford migrated. The heirs of the Durfees and Hawes and Davols and of course, Charlton, joined the names Borden and Brayton in Westport Harbor, while the Traffords, Valentines, Southards, Holts and others with close ties to the New Bedford whaling capital settled in Westport Point and Horseneck for summer enjoyment.

The bathing beach at Elephant Rock as it was known at the time was the daytime social center of Westport Harbor while the Westport Yacht Club at the Point served in a similar capacity on the other side of the river. Mothers with young children would spend hours on either the ocean or river beaches, playing in the sand and enjoying the calm waters that usually prevailed - unlike the rougher surf with a strong undertow and rip tides at nearby Horseneck Beach. Elephant Rock was considered the place to be on a warm sunny summer day, so much so that local daily newspaper, the Fall River Herald News at the beginning of the decade devoted a full page of photos of families enjoying a summer day at the beach.

Beach Rock is the nearest to shore of all the massive boulders in that stretch of shoreline and at extreme low tide, it can often be accessed without getting wet. It may have helped save the Rhee house from total destruction in 1954 as it broke the force of the ocean rushing at it from the southeast. More regularly, it served as an exciting site in the 50's for the annual July 4th bonfire.

Kids would "borrow" bales of hay from the Howland Farm and scurry along the beach collecting driftwood. All the kids participated in getting the flammable materials onto the rock. At low tide it was simple: carry it over your head. If July 4th occurred at high tide in the evening, then a rowboat was used to transport everything onto the rock. The rock is split into two sections with a narrow opening in between where the ocean sloshes below. The older kids were in charge of lighting the blaze and getting safely off the rock. Some years an accelerant was used but usually the hay was so dry that it went up in flames without any help. No one ever returned to clean up the burnt timbers that remained on the top of the rock, and the fire smell lasted well into the summer. It was as if no one knew who was responsible. Today, kids would be arrested for such an act. Oh, well!

Beach Rock with Elephant Rock in the distance.
(Photo courtesy of Paula F. Cummings)

Another large ocean rock identified as Steve's Neck actually was a name taken from what was originally the strip of land that ran from Cross Road to the east side of what is now Howland Road and the west side of Cockeset Pond to the ocean. That land mass was called Stephen's Neck in the 1770's and belonged to the Richmond family before being divided among Asa Howland (Steve's father) and Job Davis and others. And so now after two centuries, the name of the famous Richmond family that owned and settled all of Stephen's Neck is no longer found among the residents; only murmured by a small body of water named Richmond Pond.

All three large rocks, Elephant, Beach and Steve's Neck would play beneficial roles in the event that would unfold near summer's end in 1954.

While the few well-placed massive ocean rocks seemed to benefit the shoreline at Westport Harbor during major ocean storms, they also seemed to have a calming effect in general on the surf and currents along the beach compared to the neighboring beach at Horseneck. They felt, both before and after the storm to come, like quiet, stalwart sentinels.

CHAPTER 4

The Clubs

The early part of the 20th century was a very social time and our small community generated a handful of clubs to suit the residents and their idea of enjoyment. The Casino Association provided such fun. Summer residents who subscribed to the Association purchased the land on the east side of Cockeast Pond and a building called the Casino was constructed. It served to house community social events like dances, plays produced by the Westport Harbor Dramatic Club and lobster dinners. Dances with five-piece bands were held every Saturday evening, concluding at midnight.

The Harbor had its Casino and eventually the Acoaxet Club, but Horseneck also provided attractions for summer enjoyment: a dance hall, bowling alley and roller-skating rink lined East Beach at the Breakers pavilion before it was destroyed by fire in late 1920's.

Starting a yacht club in 1935 at the Point was a natural, but the economy could not have been worse. The country was still in the midst of the Great Depression but the fishing village needed a riverside location for swimming and boating instruction for kids. The adults taught children how to handle a skiff or how to sail. Parents sat on the clubhouse porch, watching their offspring jump off the float and swim in the calm waters off the beach. It was not a marina in the early days, as it has become, but a family summer gathering spot with only one dock and two floats.

While the founders of the Acoaxet Club had met 20 years earlier in the Quequechan Club in Fall River to hatch their plans, the charter members of the Westport Yacht Club were formulating their plans in the early days of the Great Depression in a tearoom at the Head of Westport owned by the mother of the May girls, Grace and Alice.

The Acoaxet Club, like the Westport Yacht Club, also experienced the Great Depression, two major hurricanes, World War II and the Korean Conflict by the time 1954 rolled around. Dwight D. Eisenhower was President and neither Alaska nor Hawaii had gained statehood. Eddie Fisher sang his hit song "Oh, My Papa" while the *Caine Mutiny*, *On the Waterfront* and *Rear Window* were the top three box office films. They could be seen in a theater but not at home on a DVD player, on television or by means of a computer. In 1954, the Acoaxet Club was the heart and soul of Westport Harbor while the Westport Yacht Club served in that capacity in Westport Point.

The weekend before Carol arrived, 21 years after the founding of the Yacht Club, the summer sailing program concluded with the annual water festival at the club just as first Commodore Clifton A. Wood had envisioned during his tenure from 1933 to 1940. Ocean races took place with gentle, variable westerly winds and Bob Kugler won first place in the Beetle Cat class and Westport Harborite Maxwell Turner won the seven-mile long handicap race despite not being a member. Outgoing Commodore John "Speech" DeNadal presented the race and season-ending prizes and conducted his term ending awards ceremony. Only a few weeks earlier at the annual meeting to elect Officers and Directors did Paul M. Kelley agree to accept the appointment as Commodore effective after Labor Day.

In 1919, when the Acoaxet Club was first conceived and Westport Harbor was being developed, the horse and buggy primarily served the area. Since it was a three-hour one-way trip from Fall River to the beach many of the prominent Fall Riverites and New Bedfordites built palatial summer "cottages" on the ocean in the Harbor and at Horseneck and East Beach to allow their families to escape the summer heat of the city. Earle Perry Charlton had the most foresight and resources as he purchased a 20-acre parcel of land on the ocean at the mouth of the harbor and river from the Sowle family in 1911.

Charlton built a new main house in 1918 after the original shingle-style mansion burned down in 1915. Then, as it is today, if an inferno starts in the Harbor it takes too long for fire apparatus to reach the site to save it. All that usually remains are the two "C's"- cellars and chimneys.

Charlton vowed to rebuild a home that would withstand all the natural elements like wind, fire, and hurricanes and called his estate "Pond Meadow". The 24 room, 9 bath room, 40,000 square foot structure was constructed of 24 inch thick granite. It is still intact in 2011. Not only did it have its own ocean and river beaches; there was a 100-foot dock for his boats. He had 4 different boats over the years and all were named *Edamena* after his wife Ida. One was loaned to the United States Coast Guard during World War I and put into service along the coastline.

Edamena IV was 99 feet long and the wharf that had been constructed by the Sowle family was long enough to accommodate her and her predecessors. In addition to the main house Charlton built other homes for his daughters, Ruth and Virginia who along with their husbands would periodically occupy them until the Great Hurricane of 1938 destroyed them. The Mitchell home on the ocean was located on Beach Avenue, where Ruth Charlton and her husband, Fritz Mitchell lived. It was a substantial brick building protected by a seawall. During the 1938 hurricane it did not leave its foundation and provided sanctuary to two maids who hid in a second floor closet. The first floor was gutted and the home damaged beyond repair. It was condemned and torn down, but foundation

Pond Meadow, before, during and after Carol.
(Photo courtesy of the Westport Historical Society)

remnants still are visible today on the beach. Fritz and Ruth later purchased the "white house" from Judge James Morton at the end of Prospect Avenue opposite the entrance to Pond Meadow. Mitchell later built the round house on the land that overlooked the river, the mouth of the harbor and the ocean, called "The Keep," to use as an office and a dark room to develop photos. Photography was his hobby. There were homes, greenhouses, large garages for automobiles and maintenance equipment as well as a carriage house and servants' quarters for gardeners, maids, butlers and chauffeurs among others. It was quite an estate and resembled a smaller version of a Newport mansion.

Earle Perry Charlton was a merchant and was often called "The Merchant Prince from Fall River". His experience as a traveling salesman as a teenager led him to meet other entrepreneurs such as Sumner Woolworth and Seymour Knox. He opened his first of many five and ten cent stores in Fall River. By 1912 he had 53 stores across the country and in Canada as chronicled by his grandson E.P. "Chuck" Charlton II in his book, The Charlton Story. Charlton sold his business to become one of the five partners of the Woolworth chain. His home was in Fall River and his summer "cottage" was in Westport Harbor. It was, and remains today, a fortress at the mouth of the harbor but is no longer owned by any family members. The main house and entire estate were sold off in 1977 for a mere $375,000, less than what it cost to build, according to Chuck Charlton in his book.

The Charlton Cup, an Acoaxet golf tournament with the final round played on Labor Day, crowns the men's golf handicap champion yearly and continues to pay tribute to the generous contribution E.P. Charlton made to the community the club serves.

Charlton continued his generosity well after his passing. In his last will and testament executed on January 2 1926, he made bequests to many of his trusted employees, including his secretary who was given $25,000 dollars and his chauffeur who inherited $10,000 - this was in the late 1920's just at the start of the depression. Five other employees each received $5,000 and four employees of the Quequechan Club in Fall River also benefited by his generosity. He also established trust funds to assist the community in perpetuity. One such fund was titled the "Charlton Charitable Trust" and was valued at two million dollars more than 80 years ago. To this date, it and other Charlton designated charitable funds provide significant support to not-for-profit organizations that serve the health, education and human service needs of area residents. Trustees, including his grandson, "Chuck," among others, oversee the funds. His will was probated in Fall River in 1930 upon his death, the same year he concluded his Acoaxet Club six-year term as president.

Charlton was not the only wealthy Westport resident at that time. The Trafford family, owners of the Westport Manufacturing Company in the north end of town adjacent to the town of Dartmouth line and Lincoln Park, built three substantial homes on East Beach. Partially constructed of beach stone, the three homes with circular drives could not survive the 1938 Hurricane and were washed away save some stone posts and fireplace bases. The four-story factory became a victim of the Depression in the 1930's and the owners never rebuilt their beachfront homes after the hurricane, according to Richie Earle, current Westport Harbormaster and a Trafford grandson. Other smaller cottages replaced the Trafford's' homes and other sizeable homes on East and West Beach after 1938 and again in 1944, only to experience Carol in 1954.

Unlike the Mitchell house and others in Westport Harbor whose foundations still rise from the sand as a testament to their existence, no such remnants can be found on East or West Beaches at Horseneck. It is as if nothing existed on either beach generations ago. We know, however, from witnesses still living and written testimony provided that was not the case as GH'38 and Carol in '54 wiped those beaches clean and took residents of those area with them to their deaths.

Besides swimming, sailing and fishing, golf was on the mind of Westport Harbor residents as Francis Ouimet, a 20 year-old Massachusetts kid from Brookline had won the 1913 United States Open Golf Championship, besting some of Europe's finest players. When the Acoaxet Club project was first undertaken, Woodrow Wilson was President of the United States and Jackson-James Frederick became the first president of the Acoaxet Club. He had served as Mayor of Fall River in the 1890's and was a noted local attorney when he accepted the presidency of the newly founded club.

Ten founding men – all with deep Fall River roots - signed the papers at the Casino in Westport Harbor to create the Acoaxet Club. They or their families had been extremely successful in Fall River when the city achieved great economic success as the world leader in the cotton business. They were all summer residents of the Harbor.

The Acoaxet Club, capitalized at $150,000 with 1,500 shares selling at $100 each, was developed gradually as money would allow; two or three golf holes at a time and when money got tight the members turned to Earle P. Charlton to replenish the coffers. E.P. advanced 50 percent of the capital needed to buy the Davis Farm and financed much of the construction of the golf course and conversion of the farmhouse into a clubhouse by matching 50 percent of the funds raised from new subscriptions. He was the second president of the Acoaxet Club from 1924 to his death in 1930. To generate more interest in golf during the club's formative years, he arranged an exhibition match in 1924 between the great Sir Walter Hagen and Joe Kirkwood Sr. Kirkwood had been the Australian, New Zealand and Canadian Open Champion. In 1924, when he joined Hagen at Acoaxet for a golf and trick shot exhibition, he had won five pro tour events that year and was the person who put Australia on the golfing map way before current Australian golf legend, Greg Norman, was even born.

Hagen was the bigger draw of the two. He was a major figure in golf in the first half of the 20th century. His tally of eleven majors is third behind Jack Nicklaus. He won the U.S. Open twice and in 1922 he became the first American to win the British Open, which he went on to win four times. Hagan also won the PGA Championship, a record tying five times between 1921 and 1927. He totaled 45 PGA wins in his career and was a six-time Ryder Cup captain. Those two living legends walking on the grass in Westport on the Acoaxet links on the fifth anniversary of its founding was certainly a motivator for members and potential members alike. Hagan's memory is still alive at Acoaxet; some young members carry Walter Hagan signature golf bags on their shoulders as they chase the ball around the track in 2010.

The club facility consisted of 165 acres of land bordered on the east by Cockeast Pond and on the west by land owned by Steve Howland on a stretch of land historically known as Stephen's Neck. It was more than enough space for a full eighteen-hole layout but it was built in phases. Unlike the neighboring Nonquit Golf Club in South Dartmouth, which did not increase its original six-hole layout until 1966, Acoaxet moved along and finished nine holes, which it remains today.

A large portion of the Acoaxet land to the north of the present facility was sold off during the Depression to neighbors as the club members could not continue to finance the project. Today, there is still a layout to the north of the present course for the second nine holes as it was envisioned nearly 100 years ago.

In 1954, there were nine golf holes, two clay tennis courts, a backboard for tennis practice but no golf practice facility. There was also a main clubhouse, which was the original farmhouse for G. Fred, son of Job, Davis. The clubhouse would become a Red Cross-like shelter to many by the end of August 1954. The main floor of the clubhouse included a dining room and kitchen along with an L-shaped living room and a small reading room just off the front hall stairs. Four guest bedrooms were located on the second floor. The third floor housed summer employees. At one point in the 1940's the space on the upper floors of the main clubhouse was where superintendent, Ed Phinney ("Hey, you kids, behave yourselves!"), his wife, Ethel, and their daughter, Susan, lived year-round. Phinney eventually was also named club professional and manager and relocated his family to an apartment over the golf pro shop and men's locker room. They resided there until their home bordering on the ninth green on lot 62 on Russell Drive was completed in 1953. The name of the road was changed in the 1960's to Fairway Drive.

Ed Phinney in his prime.
(Photo courtesy of Susan Phinney Ashworth)

Ed Phinney was hired in November 1933 as the club groundskeeper and also served as a teaching professional. Phinney was a candid instructor. On one occasion he asked his student, after hitting herself in the left ankle with a ball off a driver, if she enjoyed the game. The answer was a resounding YES! But she also wanted to improve. Phinney responded that she should "save the lesson money and just go enjoy herself." My mother took his advice and just played. An avid walker all her life she never felt that golf caused a good walk to be spoiled.

Not only did Phinney give golf lessons and run a pro shop with limited golf equipment for sale, he also provided an adequate supply of beverages and snacks. He oversaw a group of caddies and golf course helpers, and awoke many nights each week, jumped in his car or onto the tractor to manually water greens and tee boxes. On August 31, 1954, when the alarm sounded in the middle of the night, Ed rolled over and went back to sleep after hearing the torrential rain on the roof of his ranch house.

Acoaxet was built over a number of years and current designers who have walked the golf holes say that the eighth hole has the look of a Donald Ross-designed hole, but the designer remains a mystery. While the architect may never be known, the builder of the golf course is well documented and has been referenced often in this writing - he was life-long resident, farmer, developer and all-around entrepreneur, Steve Howland.

In 1953, less than a year before the arrival of a lady from the south - I am using the term "lady" loosely, of course - the Walker Cup, the international team golfing competition and amateur version of the Ryder Cup, was played at the Kittansett Club in the nearby town of Marion, only seven peninsulas to the east.

It is an 18-hole ocean links golf course. Kittansett is a native American (Wampanoag) name meaning "Near The Sea". The club maintains a measurement on its seventh-hole tee box showing the water levels from various hurricanes. Although the 1938 hurricane is generally acknowledged as the worst storm to hit southeastern Massachusetts, the water level reached at Kittanset during hurricane Carol exceeded her more notorious cousin as well as the 1944 nameless storm and Hurricane Bob in 1991, the last major tropical cyclone of any consequence to hit southeastern Massachusetts.

During the summer, Ed Phinney would replace golf club grips and polish MacGregor irons (no Nike or Cobras clubs back then) to a spit shine as well as sell and replace metal spikes on golf shoes. These odd jobs provided additional sources of revenue to him to supplement his modest club salary. On Wednesdays, his adult male member friends took the afternoon off from work and they hit the links to play a 50-cent nassau with Ed while Ethel, as she did nearly every afternoon, ran the pro shop. Ed would take an afternoon nap on

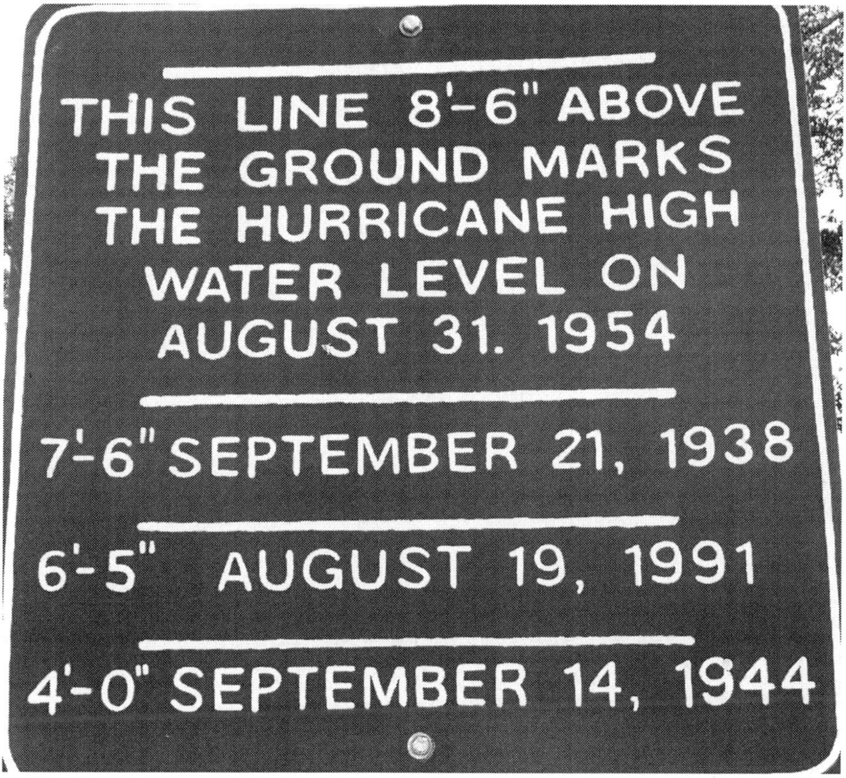
THIS LINE 8'-6" ABOVE
THE GROUND MARKS
THE HURRICANE HIGH
WATER LEVEL ON
AUGUST 31. 1954
7'-6" SEPTEMBER 21, 1938
6'-5" AUGUST 19, 1991
4'-0" SEPTEMBER 14, 1944

Kittansett 7th hole water marker

his non-golfing days to help catch up on his nightly lost sleep as a result of watering the greens and tee boxes. He was not alone in the nightly watering chores. He would assign members of his maintenance crew like "Sonny" Carter to take turns doing the same. Every two hours the location of the sprinklers would need to be rotated. During World War II, the National Guard arrested grounds crewmember, Charlie Borden, as he sped around the course at night in his car with the lights on. He was accused of sending signals to the enemy who were watching in ships off the coast. He was cleared and the next night Phinney was back on the tractor.

As course superintendent, Phinney would repair broken heavy equipment in the off-season which was often held together with bubble gum and bailing wire due to the seemingly constant financial constraints of the club. (It may have been also a prudent Yankee spending thing.) Every other Saturday evening in the summertime Phinney would don his tie and jacket and keep busy by collecting dinner/dance fees from members and guests. He would greet each new arrival in a very formal manner: "Good Evening, Mr. and Mrs. Smith." It was as if it were the first time he had seen the members all summer. He would also periodically patrol the facility to track down those who had "snuck" in the back way and "forgot" to pay at the door. A charge would appear on the forgetful member's bill at the end of the month.

Some things never change.

There were only two other buildings on the club property - a ladies locker room (prior to the early fifties it was a building where caddies were housed) and an equipment maintenance shed.

The original caddy house had been a hangout by day and sleeping quarters at night with bunk beds for caddies who had traveled from New Bedford for a summer job that paid very little when calculated on an hourly basis. After the caddy house was converted into a ladies locker room, the maintenance shed became the caddy hangout when the members' daily caddying needs had been fulfilled and additional caddies were no longer on-call.

Playing cards was the rainy day pastime for caddies and Knuckles was the game of choice. One could easily come home with no money and bloodied hands. Knuckles was a sadistic kids' card game and the non-member kids loved to send the members' kids home with bloodied paws. The goal of the game was to draw from the deck and when all the cards were selected, finish with the lowest total card value in your hand. It was a game played holding a hand of three cards and sadistic and masochistic young players rotated drawing to keep trying to select the lowest possible cards for your hand. Aces were worth only 1 point. Players take turns drawing from the deck, trying to get a 2 or a 3, or better yet an ace. As your opponent discards a card he didn't like (usually because he picked up a lower value card) you would swoop in like an osprey and pick up the card that he dropped if it was lower than a card that you already possessed. The winner got to whack the opponent's knuckles with a full deck of cards angled to impose the maximum possible pain. The total number of whacks inflicted by the winner to the losers was based upon the value of cards remaining in the losers' hands. It is not a game to play with children or grandchildren.

In fact, please do not try this at home!

The Acoaxet Club was a wonderful place for kids in spite of the game of Knuckles. Not only were there golf and tennis but social activities such as dances, bingo and various games each Monday evening during the summer. And it was one of the few local places of employment for youngsters. Horseneck, on the other hand, offered multiple summer job opportunity locations. Being a lifeguard provided many opportunities in the Horseneck vicinity while only one such job existed in the Harbor at Elephant Rock. Neither Howland's nor Foster's beach provided lifeguard services for their members and that is still the case to this date.

Caddying was big in the 50's as motorized carts were not yet in vogue and pull carts were just starting to become popular. The caddy fee was about 75 cents per bag per nine holes plus tip and drinks at the turn - the end of nine holes - and at the end of the round of 18 holes.

Your caddy was also your "go fer."

Since the Acoaxet pro shop was never far from any hole and caddies were not prohibited from carrying beer, it was part of the job to hustle back to the pro shop for refills. Dr. Dan Gallery, the first member noted in Acoaxet Board of Governors minutes for being censured for bad language, was a character who provided more laughs with every hole played. The red- faced, thinning-white-haired man was a top-notch surgeon at Truesdale Hospital in Fall River at the time. On his days off, he relaxed with Ballentine Ale or two, (or three or more.) Ballentine was the third largest brewer in the country at the time and was enjoyed by the likes of Marilyn Munroe, Joe DiMaggio, Olympian, Jim Thorpe, boxer, Rocky Marciano and Frank Sinatra as well as Dan Gallery. In later years, it was referred to as "green death" due to its hangover potential. When on the golf course, Doc took two "cold ones" with him down the first hole and by the third tee he needed two more to go. He authorized his caddy to run to the pro shop and reload while he played the short par three third and the short par four fourth hole. On the fifth tee the "Balles" in their green bottles with distinctive logo of three interlocking rings with the words: "purity, body and flavor," were waiting to keep him lubricated until he concluded the front nine holes.

Just as at all clubs, there were members at Acoaxet in the 50's who were both eccentric and memorable. Some were notorious for not being willing to spend a nickel to see an earthquake - and not just the old Yankees, either - while some members were very generous. Gallery was generous. His tips were equal to the fee per round and every caddie hoped for a loop with Doc.

Ed Phinney arrived at Acoaxet five years before the big hurricane of 1938, so he knew the potential devastation of a major tropical storm. He'd seen first hand the substantial oceanfront cottages that had been totally destroyed and he could still see the remaining house foundations along the south facing beachfront. He'd heard the terrible experiences some of his club members had lived through.

However, every hurricane is different. Since Phinney and his family were year-round residents, they had experienced strong northeast winter storms and had seen the ocean water break through the beach and cross Atlantic Avenue forming an inlet into Cockeast Pond. He had seen the waters of the brackish Cockeast Pond rise onto three holes of the golf course-five, six and eight. He'd witnessed heavy limbs snap off mighty chestnut trees around the clubhouse, seen shingles tear from roofs, and fences collapse while experiencing winds in excess of 125 miles per hour. He'd watched homes wash up onto the golf course and telephone poles join uprooted trees on their sides. Phinney had seen unmanned pond boats rushing north into Cockeast Pond. But the pro would see more devastation and physical chaos in late August of 1954 than ever before.

He knew that August 31, 1954 was another "big one."

There had been no specific hurricane warnings on August 31. As the wind raged and the rain came down sideways, Ed Phinney and his crew worked doggedly to shore up the buildings and grounds of the Acoaxet Club. They moved about the property not aware that they were in the middle of a major hurricane, as they, like others, had no warning or knowledge of the events about to unfold when they arrived for work at 6 a.m. They secured the various gutters that were coming off the pro shop and checked into the clubhouse periodically to see how the houseguests and assorted neighbors from low-lying properties were faring in the unsanctioned Red Cross-like shelter.

He updated the inhabitants on the outside activity. With him were four of his crewmembers: William "Sonny" Carter from nearby Little Compton, teenager Jimmy Lawrence and caddy master Richard Lake, both from Adamsville, and Dale Plante, a scrappy six-foot, 150-pound, teenager, who lived with relatives during the summer in Tiverton, Rhode Island. Carter was Ed's assistant and the only nearly year-round (nine-month) employee. He was 29 and had already worked 13 years with Phinney as a caddy and a maintenance assistant. In 1957, Sonny moved on from his $35-a-week job at Acoaxet to become the Superintendent at Foxborough Country Club at $75 a week. He later returned to Acoaxet for nearly 10 years to work on the grounds and finally retired at the turn of the century.

Young, bespectacled Dale Plante joined his twin brother, Dana, who worked on the other side of Cockest Pond at the Harbor Inn/Ogden's Store. (They were not related to the Plante family who owned and operated Plante's Pavilion on Horseneck beach that would also experience the terrible effects of the storm.) Dana, who worked in the store and lived at the Inn in the summer for three years, was scheduled for a day off and generally took the bus back to a relative's house in Tiverton for the day. The twins were 17 years old at the time and their mother had separated the brothers' living arrangements so they could establish their own identities, as she had told them. Less than

Dale (l) and Dana Plante
(Photo courtesy of Dale Plante)

(Postcard courtesy of Albert E. Lees Jr. collection)

two months earlier at the end of the school year Dana, a student at Case High in Swansea, had received the Harvard Book Prize presented to high school juniors by the Harvard Club of Fall River. The twins found summer jobs at the Acoaxet Club and the Harbor Inn in Westport Harbor. Acoaxet Club golf professional/greenskeeper Ed and his wife, Ethel Phinney treated Dale, who worked primarily in the pro shop and on the grounds, like a son, according to Dale, who went on to study at the University of Massachusetts. Dale resided with relatives on River Road in the Harbor. Dana found everyone who worked and /or who visited Ogden's Store also very welcoming. Their lives, however, were nearly shattered and turned upside down on August 31, 1954.

CHAPTER 5

Oggies

The Cozy Cab bus from Fall River made two daily round trips to Westport Harbor with stops at the Harbor Inn or Ogden Store, as it was also known in the 1950's. There were two United States Postal pick-ups per day at the Acoaxet Post Office, which was housed on the first floor in the caged-in south end section of the store – complete with about 60 post office boxes. The entire space with its wooden floor and low ceiling was painted a pale shade of green, a popular color in Westport homes and businesses in the 50's.

The next stop to the south of the facility would be Westport, Ireland, so if your horse needed oats or your vehicle needed gasoline, Macomber Brothers, later known as Harbor Inn/Ogden's Store, was the end of the trip. Macombers/The Harbor Inn/Ogden's Store and United States Post Office trace their roots back to the 1800's. Two businesses grew out of the need to service horses and their drivers as well as passengers. In the 1860's, the Westport Harbor stagecoach line that was operated by Charlie Macomber made rail and ship connections with Fall River, Massachusetts, approximately 20 miles north. At 10 a.m. daily, the Fall River stagecoach departed for its three-hour, one-way trip to the city. Hay was the fuel of choice in the early years, but was replaced by gasoline when the horse-drawn carriage was replaced by a large touring car that Macomber purchased to transport his customers. The blue Sunoco gas pumps (now painted white) can still be seen. This gas and motor oil outlet was always spartan-no Green Stamps, coffee mugs or dishes with the sale of gas like other service stations did at the time and no oil checks unless requested, and patrons were on their own to wash their windshields.

(Postcard courtesy of Albert E. Lees Jr. collection)

The Macomber brothers, Charlie and Arthur, bought the functioning dairy and crop farm located in the fields around Perch Rock where River and Acoaxet roads merge. They then added a thriving livery and boarding stable. By 1894 the enterprise included a grocery store, post and telegraph office, wagon repair and freight hauling trade. During this time the facility also served as a stable and horse-boarding area providing care for the horses of summer residents. That space subsequently became the general store and post office.

Less than a quarter mile away, overlooking the harbor where the ocean rushes into the mouth of the Westport River, was the Sowle Seaside Hotel, which had enjoyed major success as a vacation retreat in the second half of the 19th century. It is said that Harriet Beecher Stowe, author of Uncle Tom's Cabin, spent vacation time at the Sowle Hotel among other Westport locations. By the end of the century, Captain Sowle passed on, and a fire destroyed part of the structure. The Macomber Brothers bought the three story south wing of the Sowle Hotel and moved it less than a quarter of a mile west to adjoin their main building to consolidate it with their other businesses.

They did not fear hurricane damage since the last severe hurricane to hit Westport was in 1815. Multiple ocean storms sideswiped Westport over the next century but none ever caused significant damage until 1938.

The brothers incorporated the inn into the north side of their structure. By 1907, the Harbor Inn was functioning under the direction of the Macombers. It was a Textron-like conglomerate ahead of its time.

And while Acoaxet had Oggies, other sections of Westport had mirror image businesses.

The Hammonds ran a similar operation on Main Road in the Point complete with a post office, and general store with a gas pump out front. On Horseneck, the John Alden Store also housed a post office for years in the early part of the 20th century. It was located behind the Surfside Hotel along East Beach. The Kingfisher House on East Beach Road at Horseneck, although destroyed in the '38 hurricane, was the most similar to the Harbor Inn/Ogden's Store. It was an inn, and sold groceries as well as cold drinks and ice cream, candy and special treats.

Charlie Macomber had one child, a daughter, Miriam, who married a fellow by the name of Herman Ogden. After Charlie Macomber retired as Postmaster, Herman took over as Postmaster and general manager. Prior to that, he owned a Buick automobile dealership in Fall River that had failed during the Great Depression. Herman enjoyed the non-postal aspects of running the enterprise, which thrived each year with the arrival of the summer community. He enjoyed stocking the store with Monarch and SS Pierce brand groceries and even provided delivery service in the Acoaxet area. His daughter, Peggy, would often ride her bicycle from home to home with orders filled at the store. During World War II, Mr. Ogden worked at the naval station in Newport, Rhode Island, and tended to the store's dealings each evening. The workload seemingly became too much and he died at age 49 within a year of his father–in-law, Charlie. It was then that Miriam took over the conglomerate. She did that for more than 30 years, post-marking and inserting the mail into local patrons boxes until she retired and sold the establishment in 1975. (The Macomber/Ogden family felt the post office belonged to their family, since they were the only ones who ever operated it. That was the end of both the store and the post office, as the new owners only wanted to run an inn on the site.)

Upon entering the store on your immediate right were the ice cream freezers and the large bright red "Coca Cola" soda cooler that could be opened on top from both front and back. Circulating ice-cold water kept the bottled (no cans or plastic back then) Coke, cream soda, Moxie, and other thirst-quenching beverages cold and the hands of the clerk, who refilled the machine, numb. Next to the five-cent sodas and ice cream (the price was also a nickel per scoop in a cone or box for the six best-selling flavors) were Fudgesicles, Popsicles and other cold treats such as Hoodsie Cups, which were supplied twice weekly by the Hood milk driver who also provided products to the stores at the Point and around Horseneck.

There was an abundance of penny candy in the glass case from which to choose, including Mary Janes, Squirrels, and Red Hot Dollars, red and black licorice, Bazooka Bubble Gum and more. It was a store clerk's nightmare as kids lined up for "one candy cigarettes and two wax bottles with sugar colored water inside. No, not that. Make it one of these. No, I'll have… and charge that eight cents to my parents account."

Above the freezer housing icy treats was the cigarette display: Camels, Lucky Strikes, Pall Malls and all the best non-filter cancer sticks one could ever desire. Throughout the store there was bread, milk and staples like toilet paper and other items in case of emergency. Beach toys and sand pails were next to the magazine rack with weekly and daily summer reading selections and a complete supply of romance comic books. The rotating wire stand for postcards of area scenes of Westport selling at five cents each or three for a dime was as prominent as were fishing supplies like line, weights, and hooks.

Cash was accepted but most items were on a charge account basis including the penny candy. The customer's name was written on the top of the sheet and a running list was kept until the page was complete. Then a new sheet was created. Often times the same customer had running sheets on multiple pads. Every sheet was carbonized. The top copy was inserted into the customer's mailbox as a monthly statement and Miriam retained the other half for her accounts receivable records that she managed from her oak roll top desk (coveted by many summer visitors) in the post office.

Sunday was the most chaotic day for the store that was open more than twelve hours daily from June through September. Ice cream was packaged for Sunday lunch and newspapers were sorted and assembled in the early morning in the large open storage room behind the store proper for pick up by 7:30 a.m. Customers, both paying and non-paying, could access the "paper room" from the parking area next to the gas pumps in front of the store. The doors were kept open most of the day, everyday, to improve air circulation in the store which was located on the ground level below the high point of the land to the south. There were large stable-size doors that opened to provide easy admission and also allow kids to gain entrée to the empty NuGrape bottles waiting to be picked up by the distributor. Since the empties were redeemable at two cents each, the trip through the stable doors back outside and into the front door of the store was worthwhile. The resulting redemption translated into a free Charleston Chew–the dentist's favorite - or even a Creamsicle for a young bandit.

One could retrieve one's mail or drop out-going letters in the slot but no formal postal activity was conducted on the Lord's Day. Sand pails, kites and Pinky rubber balls were big Sunday sellers. Parking was available in the back of the store for one dollar a day for day-trippers who could then walk down Boathouse Row and enjoy a day at the Charlton's Wharf beach on the river.

At Oggies, if you needed it, you could get it. And as the staff would say;

"If we don't have it, you don't need it."

What has disappeared over the years from the front of the building is the pay telephone booth. The glass booth with the accordion door for privacy was the only one in the Harbor, ever. Kids had a dime in their pocket to call home in case of emergency.

Guests at the 30-room inn with its maze of hallways and staircases (many had heavy rope as handrails) arrived and departed, but by the mid 50's, not with great frequency. The dozen or so guest rooms were mainly located in the Sowle Hotel wing on the north side of the structure. On the first floor, a small sitting room with a bar served as an early evening gathering spot for inn guests to enjoy a beverage and recount the day's activities. Some of the bedrooms enjoyed the privacy of a toilet room inside what was formerly a closet. Other rooms shared a toilet room located in the hallway. The bedrooms were equipped with an oak dresser and nightstand with a lamp, either a double or twin beds with horsehair mattresses and a chamber pot for late-night emergencies. A common dining area lured guests for breakfast and dinner with homemade food prepared on the enormous cast iron stove. In years past, this area was the hayloft over the stables below.

Mrs. Ogden oversaw the entire operation including the staff of high school kids who worked behind the counter but were not allowed in the post office - "federal regulation" everyone was told. Generally, Mrs. Ogden, who was a slight woman, stood at the counter near the safe and the cash register with a Pall Mall lipstick encrusted cigarette dangling out of her mouth. Her daughter, Peggy, maintained that she never learned how to inhale. She was always properly attired in a full-length dress and bright red lipstick. A glass of clear liquid, which was constantly being refreshed, sat behind the support pole near the quahog shells that she used as ashtrays for the half-smoked cigarettes. The permanent staff included Eunice Townsend, a tall thin African-American cook from California who lived and worked in the inn during the summer season and the teenagers who oversaw the counter purchases and pumped gasoline from the two tanks-high test and regular-in front of the store. Housekeeping functions were performed by Suzie Sisson, a four foot gnome-like woman with a heart of gold, who lived on Adamsville Road about six miles away.

The modern day "Oggies" provided a pit stop for Jimmy Graham, the bus driver, and others traveling to and from Westport Harbor. Cozy Cab maintained a livery service to Acoaxet for many years as the motor coach's destination shield above the front window proclaimed. Eunice was one of the frequent weekly passengers on the vehicle to Fall River and was often joined on the rides by other domestics on their days off for a trip to the city to do some shopping.

On occasions local kids would implore Jimmy to give them a ride on his route from Oggies to the Acoaxet Club about two miles away. It was not so much that the kids were lazy but the fun of the ride surpassed all expectations. Jimmy agreed to do this on days when he had no paying customers but he was often seen parked at the end of Brayton Point Road (not on his route) overlooking the ocean with a young woman on board who had traveled with him for a day trip from Fall River.

Mary Ann McGowan 1953
(Photo courtesy of Mary McGowan O'Toole)

On August 31,1954, it was not Eunice's day off, but it was Dana Plante's. At the time he was one of the high school kids working at Mrs. Ogden's at below government approved hourly pay rates. He boarded the bus around 10 a.m. joining another teenager already seated, named Mary McGowan.

Mary was returning from her home in Somerset, Massachusetts, the suburban town just a short ride over the Taunton River to the bus terminal in Fall River. She was heading to her live-in babysitting job in Westport Harbor near the Acoaxet Club. Mary had enjoyed her day off with her family but her trip down from Fall River to Ogden's store had been increasingly unnerving. McGowan and Plante did not know each other but they were in for a trip of a lifetime!

After a brief stop it was time for Jimmy, the well-known driver, and his two paying customers on his 28-seat passenger vehicle to proceed on their trip. Jimmy went inside to use the facilities, grabbed a Moxie from the cooler and took a box of Good N' Plenty with him for sustenance. Mary stayed on-board believing she only had a few more minutes before she arrived at her stop on Howland Road while Dana was just beginning his journey. They drove down Acoaxet Road a few hundred feet, bearing right onto Atlantic Avenue for a three-quarter mile stretch of ocean front road along the barrier beach. At the end of Atlantic Avenue, the road made a turn to the right onto Howland Road toward the Acoaxet Club, then on to Adamsville and back to Fall River. The sand on the bathing beach at Elephant Rock along Atlantic Avenue was just starting to rise from ground level, creating dunes that had been flattened in 1938 and again in 1944. The dunes were not so high to prevent a view of the water from a passing vehicle or even from a bicycle but restoration of the dune height was slow progress. All on board the bus could see the ferocious waves breaking over the low dunes as they approached the Elephant Rock Beach Club pavilion.

Mrs. Ogden's only child, Margaret "Peggy" Ogden Cowing, was brought up in the Harbor Inn and had witnessed the massive 1938 hurricane followed in 1944 by one less severe. By 1954, she had seen enough storms, but Carol, succeeded by Edna only 11 days later, brought the community to its knees and placed her home and her mother's livelihood on an island in Westport Harbor. Peggy wrote in her journal, "the Harbor was a wild, thrilling place during the hurricane, needless to say. Other than that I shall write no more."

– Part Two –

CHAPTER 6

The Long Island Express

Then up and spake an old sailor
Had sailed the Spanish Main,
"I pray thee, put in yonder port
For I fear a hurricane."

"The Wreck of the Hesperus"
H.W. LONGFELLOW

Hurricane season begins on the first of June each year and concludes on the last day of November. The warmth of the Atlantic Ocean often dictates the results. In the early part of the season, the warm water currents bring the storms from the lower Atlantic into the Caribbean and the Gulf of Mexico. By mid-season, the water temperature in the Northern Atlantic encourages storms to sweep up the coastline while at the same time wind currents can blast storms into Florida (Hurricane Andrew) or then into the Gulf Coast (Katrina) with incredible intensity. The strength of most recent storms is blamed on global warming by some while others disavow the concept entirely. In recent history, the average number of storms per year in the Atlantic is 11 but some years it has grown to as many as seventeen. However, over the past 20 years or so, very few have reached the colder waters of the New England coast. In fact, only Hurricane Gloria in 1985 and Bob in 1991 reached the New England coastline in approximately the last 40 years.

1954 was different. But Carol was certainly not the first hurricane to slam New England. "The Great New England Hurricane of

1938" sometimes dubbed "The Long Island Express" or "GH 38" was still fresh in the minds of most in New England. It reached landfall with wind gusts of 183 miles per hour. As with Carol in 1954, there was little or no warning provided to residents of New England coastal towns and with a storm surge of 10 to 12 feet of water it inundated parts of Narragansett and Buzzards Bays. In Westport Harbor, approximately 45 summer cottages built along the stretch of beach referred to as Elephant Rock Beach were in danger. Thirty-six were totally destroyed and another 5 were partially destroyed or moved from their foundations. As well as the beachfront being wiped out, 10 of the 11 boathouses on the riverfront also succumbed. On West Beach and East Beach at Horseneck more than 100 homes were destroyed. The main difference between the 1938 Hurricane and Hurricane Carol? The date and time of arrival.

The storm of 1938 arrived well after the height of the summer season when summer folk with children had gone back to school and it was mostly parents with pre-school age children and grandparents who enjoyed the late, quiet summer season. It also arrived late in the day and into the dark of night on September 21st.

That was the good news and the only good news. The bad news was that the most dangerous part of the '38 hurricane, the right quadrant, would pass right over Rhode Island and Westport on its way northward. A fast-moving storm, passing 425 miles in less than seven hours or moving at nearly 60 miles per hour; it arrived on the Westport shore around 3 p.m. and took 3 hours to pass. It was a freak, said many, as they picked through the debris. But no, apparently, it was no fluke.

Unlike a microburst, a type of downburst wind (often at speeds over 100 miles per hour) that affects an area two and a half miles in diameter or less, a hurricane touches a wide area over a much longer period of time. Both have major destructive powers. A hurricane provides a warning time frame while a microburst, however, strikes without warning and vanishes just as rapidly. Hurricanes gain their strength from warm waters while a microburst feeds off a thunderstorm and is more common over land such as the heartland of this country.

Like a microburst, a tornado is also spawned from a thunderstorm and is called nature's most violent storm. It devastates neighborhoods in seconds, even entire towns like Xenia, Ohio described by Polk Laffoon in his book, Tornado. Winds can exceed 300 miles per hour and create damage paths one mile wide and 50 miles long as they did in the southern states in April 2011. The most destructive tornado ever occurred in Alabama in 2011 with hundreds dead and missing. Occasionally, a tornado will travel over water such as Narragansett Bay in Rhode Island, creating a waterspout with little or no warning, with the funnel cloud appearing in late afternoon or early evening at the tail end of a summer thunderstorm.

A tsunami, on the other hand, is the result of an earthquake under water. The wave can travel hundreds of miles at hundreds of miles per hour before its effects are felt on land. The water can engulf and drown hundreds of thousands of low-lying inhabitants as it did in the Indian Ocean event of 2004 and again in Japan in 2011 before people realized what was happening. The earthquakes recorded at approximately 9.0 magnitudes at the epicenter, which was the equivalent of the energy released by 23,000 Hiroshima–type atomic bombs according to the U.S. Geological Survey. Hundreds of thousand of people were swallowed up without warning, never to be seen or heard from again.

While tornados, micro bursts and tsunamis are potential killer weather strikes, weather experts view hurricanes as the most violent weather phenomena. "But a hurricane is the most intense weather system on earth", according to Elizabeth Ritchie, Associate Professor in the Departments of Science and Electrical and Computer Engineering at the University of Arizona.

The toll in 1938 was heavy. Eighty-four lives were lost including 22 lives lost in Westport. Nineteen died at Horseneck and three from Westport Harbor. Gulls, seafowl and salt spray were blown inland as far north as Burlington, Vermont, and strange tropical birds were seen locally. There were rumors at the time of 40-foot tidal waves but according to Richard K. Hawes, Esquire, who experienced the storm on the shore at Westport Harbor and wrote about it in his essay The Hurricane at Westport Harbor, there were in fact three surges. The last and largest occurred around 5:45 p.m. That one topped off at about two feet below the head of Elephant Rock. She produced a storm surge at Westport Harbor in excess of 14 feet. In his account penned only six days following the event, Hawes noted the warmth of the water and wrote: "the air was so filled with spray and rain driven horizontally with flying shingles, that it was difficult to look windward or see very much of anything going on in the ocean. Houses, which were uninsured, just floated away and collapsed from the turbulence and force of the rising water and speed of the wind-driven short steep waves." He noted that all the cottages from the Point of Rocks at the mouth of the Harbor across the mile-long beachfront to Brayton Point were "completely swept away or damaged beyond repair with the exception of two." Hawes noted that "the hurricane struck without warning and the rise of the water at its climax was extremely rapid; so rapid in fact that those who were in houses between the ocean and the pond were trapped beyond rescue."

The impact was felt across the continent. The added depth of water on our North Atlantic coast caused recordings on the seismograph at Sitka, Alaska, according to John W. Cummings 2nd, Esquire in his writing, Hurricanes into Hop. At 5:45 p.m. the weather data read: barometer 29.09 degrees (indicating the approach of high winds and bad weather) with wind south east at 105 miles per hour and gusts recorded at 115 miles per hour. The air temperature was 80 degrees with high tide due at 6:47 p.m. and there was a new moon set to rise. None of this data boded well for Westport residents and their property in the hours to come.

Of the 22 Westport victims who lost their lives in GH 38 only seven were Westport residents while the balance were summer visitors. The oldest was 89 and the youngest was two. Three hundred seventeen died in nearby Rhode Island while in Westport Harbor, Mary Frances Black, 43, who was the Mills family cook, drowned. Her charge that day was young Betty Mills, also known as Wee Anne,

Harold Barker's "Harbor" house succumbs to GH 38
(Photo courtesy of Westport Historical Society)

12 years old at the time, who was washed out of the house with Miss Black by a wave while watching the ocean from the family beachfront house window. They both landed in Cockeast Pond, a foreboding of future events. Betty saved herself by floating on debris and then swimming full tilt until finally landing on the fifth hole on the golf course, a site where others would find themselves deposited 16 years later. She swam ashore after disrobing, realizing she could not make it through the heavy reeds fully attired. She trudged through the dense underbrush to safety while Miss Black was washed to her death on the east side of Gull Rock in the pond. She was last seen holding onto a pole.

Wee Ann was taken to Truesdale Hospital in Fall River and was treated for exposure. Betty never spoke publicly about this horrifying experience. In 1988, when the Acoaxet Club hosted an event to note the 50th anniversary of the hurricane, Betty still could not attend nor relate the events or in particular her own terrifying experience. She sent her husband, Frank Coolidge, to tell her story. She often warned her three children to "have 100 percent respect for the ocean" but because the event traumatized her so much, she never spoke about it even at home, her son, Frank Junior, related in 2009.

The Mills family story did not end on the day of the hurricane or the following days when their daughter was hospitalized and their maid was buried. Ten years later, a member of the Acoaxet Club, while playing golf, discovered a diamond ring on the eighth hole. That was the hole where the remnants of the Mills oceanfront home settled. The ring bore the initials of Mrs. Mills. The ring that her husband had given her was returned to her finger a decade after it had been lost.

Mary Black was not the only resident of Westport Harbor to die in GH38: Edith McNabb, 68, a widow, whose home was next to the Mitchell house on the beach within a hundred yards of the Point of

Rocks, and her housekeeper, 21–year-old Helen Almy, were also victims when the beach and all Westport beaches were swept clean.

It was the perfect storm. But not the last.

The significant loss of life in '38 was attributed to the lack of warning, preparation and the absence of a great hurricane hitting the area in most anyone's memory that was alive at the time. One person, Oliver Wilcox who lived in Middletown, Rhode Island, maintained that GH38 was not as severe as the last hurricane he lived through in 1869 when he was 17 years old.

Those who were still in Westport after Labor Day were grandparents or parents of those with pre-school age children. If the storm had struck before Labor Day, the loss of life would have been significantly higher. Since they had not experienced a hurricane, those who were enjoying the September warmth and temperate water temperature assumed the increasing wind was simply another gale force windstorm that would require boats to be secured and bathing suits taken off the clothesline. They would then settle in for the evening and experience the wonders of the weather at the oceanfront. But that was not to be. Despite their efforts to protect their homes by boarding up windows and constructing barricades of sand bags, that sometimes are successful in holding back flood waters, neither provides protection from the waves of the ocean during a hurricane. Their efforts were futile.

By the following day when the sun came out there was nothing left on the beaches in Westport. The homes in the Harbor, on Horseneck and East Beach were nothing but sand and rock. Rock and concrete foundations were visible in the Harbor but the wooden structures were washed away, miles away, in some cases. As Everett

Allen described it in his book, A Wind To Shake The World, "What I saw was a waste-land of sand and stone with not one stick left of the scores and scores of buildings that line the shore. Even the paved road was gone." And further on in his first hand account of what he witnessed at Horseneck, "The scene was repeated at West Beach. Miles of summer places - from small cottages to large residences of seasonal visitors - smashed from their foundations and the debris was carried by mountainous waves into salt marshlands and sand dunes."

Carlton "Cukie" Macomber lived through every hurricane since GH38. His research showed that before '38 there were 113 houses on East Beach, many year round homes of substantial size - he termed them: "mansions, huge houses." But after September 21, 1938, they were all gone. Cukie recalls in the publication titled, Westport Experiences-the Dark Side of Nature -The Hurricane of 1938 published by students at Westport High School, "I think there were two buildings left on East Beach; also before the hurricane, the land between the beach and the road was quite extensive." He continued, "Where the mansions were, there must have been 500 feet of flat ground before you got to the beach. Down on East Beach today you can't find a place with 100 feet. That's how much has disappeared." Cukie's father maintained an auto repair business and had to struggle through the Great Depression to stay solvent but he had friends who were not so fortunate. Charley and Alma Sowle operated a restaurant and gift shop on East Beach. They also had a one armed bandit in the back room. The couple worked hard all summer but deferred paying their bills until the end of the season. On September 21, 1938 Charley dropped off Alma at the Macomber house for a visit while he went on the Fall River to pay the bills. After paying his auto bill at the Macomber Repair Shop, he encouraged Alma to join him and head home. The wind had started to blow hard but this did not deter Charley who had experienced many a local storm. Cukie's mother was the last person to see them alive.

Former Fall River Mayor, James H. Kay, maintained a home on the beach at Horseneck. He and his wife, Mary, tried to evacuate but their car flooded out and they were trapped, according to their grandson, Jim Kay in the Westport High School student publication. When they saw what they believed was a tidal wave coming, they sought refuge in a small cottage across the road. When the wave hit, their house was demolished. "They climbed into the attic of the small cottage and hung over the rafters all night. The whole house picked up and floated into the marsh," reported Kay. Everyone survived but as it turned out, the Mayor had suffered a heart attack. Jim's grandmother would never sleep near the ocean again; she could not stand the roar of the waves.

Others rode out the storm on the roofs of their houses as they floated up river. Those who did, like Mayor Kay, survived to tell their stories. Others were stubborn and simple hunkered down. Some made it. Many did not. As many as 50 people sought refuge in the high dunes as others did during Carol years later, according to Bill Tripp, owner of F.L. Tripp and Sons Boat Yard. Tripp reported that the water rose five feet in the boat yard, which was one foot less than Carol 16 years later. Tripp has seen many hurricanes in his 84 years and he says, "If you've seen one hurricane, you've really seen all you need to see."

Things were no different in Westport Harbor. There was tragedy. There was destruction. There were survival stories.

Richard K. Hawes, Jr., Esquire, son of attorney R.K. Hawes who wrote, The Hurricane at Westport Harbor told the Westport High students for their publication that the beach along Atlantic Avenue known as Elephant Rock Beach had sand dunes similar to, but smaller than, Horseneck before the storm. "They were flattened," he reported. "There was nothing where all the houses had been. The beach was torn up. The ocean had churned up the road. It was all gone," he said. "What had been a whole summer community of people was gone," said the Fall River attorney whose roots go deep in Acoaxet. He recalled that only one or two people had the nerve, or lack of good sense, to build back on the beach after the storm.

The most chilling of the many storm-related stories came from the Blakney family who had spent 20 years in their East Beach cottage. James Blakney was a former Fall River resident who spent half the year in Florida and the balance at his East Beach home. He and his wife had seen many seasonal ocean storms and gave little thought to this one. He put his auto in a friend's garage, which was destroyed; the car was found in a ditch and determined to be totally worthless.

As the storm intensified, Blakney and his wife realized that their efforts to protect their cottage were in vain as the water began sweeping through it, rather than under it. They made a break for it and headed across the road to another house that looked stronger. As he left his house, he was asked by a stranger to help get the stranger's mother and son to safety. The water had such force that the three strangers were separated from each other as the man's mother's dress was torn off and the son became separated from Blakney's grasp. Could a similar event occur at the same area in 1954?

The Blakney's made it across the street after a struggle and forced open a rear door to the vacant home. It was not long, however, before they needed to seek another location for shelter as the house they were in was knocked off its foundation and they found themselves in three feet of water.

"I noticed that the chimney was beginning to buckle and sought to get to the stairs of a nearby cottage", Blakney reported to The Herald News on September 23, 1938. He continued, "The cottage we were in was swept along for a distance of about a mile and then it swung around. I grabbed a three by four 12 foot post and used it for a pole, hanging onto it until the house started to break up…I saw the roof of my own cottage coming at us. We crossed it and the roof of another house and then picked up another board and used it to cross a third roof." Finally, upon reaching land, the couple fought through brush and bramble, walked miles and then found safety inland. "We noticed one couple making a raft of beds inside their home, piling one on top of another until they nearly touched the ceiling," he concluded. It is not known who they were and if they survived, but homes were found over two miles away on the river shoreline. The Blakney experience lasted for nearly three hours until nightfall.

The New Bedford Standard Times edition of Saturday, October 1, 1938, reported that survivors claimed waves 20 feet high at Horseneck and many West Beach residents survived because they found refuge in the high sand dunes while East Beach people like Blakney were trapped between the ocean and The Let of the river where the water merged into one body of water. The news story read, "So complete was the demolition of cottages in most places the owners had difficulty finding the wreckage of their homes. Large pavilions and stores at summer resorts met the same fate. Built only a few feet above sea level, these structures were engulfed by surging waters and torn to pieces."

In her book, Sudden Sea - The Great Hurricane of 1938, author R.A. Scotti noted, "In Massachusetts the shore of Buzzards Bay was little more than wreckage. One complete house was still standing in ritzy Westport Harbor." Although Scotti was not totally accurate-there were only very few homes which survived the storm's destructive force.

Less than six years later on September 14, 1944, another no-name hurricane zeroed in on the area. A hurricane plane spotted a violent storm off Puerto Rico, which had all the ingredients to duplicate GH38. A cold front from the north due to arrive on September 13 was expected to re-route the storm out to sea but it did not arrive in time and the cyclone entered the Rhode Island Sound before midnight. The weather authorities considered this storm to be the most violent in history with a barometer reading of 26.85" and a forward speed that carried it 400 miles to New England in eleven hours. The 100-mile-per-hour storm arrived late at night but fortunately the loss of life was minimal due to early radio and newspaper warnings. People had vivid memories of '38 and vacated waterfront homes early in the day. The storm on September 14, 1944, had considerably less human impact since most families had returned to winter homes as school had started. Those who had not left were invited to do so by Civil Defense, State Guard or Coast Guard reservists by 7 p.m. Eight residents of Westport Harbor living on Remington Avenue near the Elephant Rock Beach Club were removed from their home by a Coast Guard unit late that evening. Fortunately, the tide was nearly low at midnight in the Westport area during the peak of the storm when winds exceeded 105 miles per hour. The community was spared from another brutal beating. Rainfall totaled 5.56" in the 24-hour period. The barometer read 28.53," which was .56" lower than GH38. But because the storm struck just before low tide the water level was only 3.5 feet above mean high water.

That is not to say that the damage to property was insignificant. The high water from the surge collapsed homes and businesses from Westport beaches to Cape Cod and the Islands. Buildings folded and radio towers toppled. Roadways washed out while trees uprooted and utility poles prevented passage on streets. Boats landed on docks, in yards and on roads. Remnants of homes were piled like matchsticks in marshes. Buildings were moved off their foundations. Again, East Beach in Westport was wiped clean. Homes on West Beach at Horseneck also sustained major damage, but, like Westport Harbor, there were now fewer homes left on the beachfront. However, utility crews found the damage to their lines much greater than in '38 as there were now miles more lines and cables to repair six years later.

"Though GH38 was quickly crowded off the front pages outside New England by the drums of war in Europe, it would never be forgotten as the time the public in New England came to understand that large events, bad things beyond their making, could strike even on their doorstep," wrote Cherrie Burns in her written account, The Great Hurricane 1938.

Just like its predecessor, GH38 and it's successor, the 1944 Hurricane in Westport, Carol washed up debris, cast boats high and dry onto land, destroyed fishing fleets, tore roofs off homes and caused financial ruin for many.

But GH38 had taught lessons. Fewer homes were rebuilt on the waterfront. Those that were came with major improvements to withstand wind and water. There was also a new respect for advanced warnings, which saved lives and that was the best possible outcome for the 1944 Hurricane in Westport.

While there was no formal name for the 1938 or 1944 hurricanes were occasionally named according to the National Hurricane Center,

"For several hundred years, hurricanes in the West Indies were often named after the particular saint's day on which the hurricane occurred. For example, "Hurricane San Felipe" struck Puerto Rico on 13 September 1876. Another storm struck Puerto Rico on the same day in 1928, and this storm was named "Hurricane San Felipe the Second." Later, latitude-longitude positions were used. However, experience has shown that using distinctive names in communications is quicker and less subject to error than the cumbersome latitude longitude identification methods. Using women's names became the practice during World War Two following the use of a woman's name for a storm in the 1941 novel "Storm" by George R. Stewart. In 1951, the United States adopted a confusing plan to name storms by a phonetic alphabet (Able, Baker, Charlie), and in 1953 the nation's weather services returned to using female names. The practice of using female names exclusively ended in 1978 when names from both genders were used to designate storms in the eastern Pacific. A year later, male and female names were included in lists for the Atlantic and Gulf of Mexico. The name lists, which have been agreed upon at international meetings of the World Meteorological Organization, have a French, Spanish, Dutch, and English flavor because hurricanes affect other nations and are tracked by the public and weather services of many countries." The Tropical Prediction Center in Miami, Florida keeps a constant watch on oceanic storm-breeding grounds. Once a system with counterclockwise circulation and wind speeds of thirty-nine miles per hour or greater is identified, the Center gives the storm a name from the list for the current year. The letters Q, U, X, Y, and Z are not included because of the scarcity of names beginning with those letters. Names associated with storms that have caused a significant death toll and/or damage are usually retired from the list."

Refugees from GH38 recover personal effects at Horseneck.
(Photo courtesy of New Bedford Standard Times)

By 1954 the Weather Bureau was naming hurricanes. One of the first was named "Hurricane Dog." Thankfully, "Dog" never dumped on land but still holds the record for the longest continuation of a category five- the most intense and dangerous - hurricane. The scale is based upon a one to five rating and it is called the Saffir - Simpson Hurricane Wind Scale. A sustained wind of 155 miles per hour as is the case of a category five is expected to produce catastrophic damage, including complete roof and, in some cases, building failures. Nearly all trees and power poles will be snapped or uprooted. Power outages will last for weeks, perhaps even months.

Hurricanes have never been particularly selective about where they made landfall. Florida, however, with its warm summertime waters, seems to attract the most uninvited guests. The fact that the state could be attacked from both the Atlantic Ocean and the Gulf of Mexico allows for more storms to enter than other locales. The warm waters of the Gulf have produced multiple storms and incredible damage to the states of Louisiana, Texas and Mississippi.

On the east coast of the United States, South Carolina and North Carolina have also been ravaged more than their fair share. Due to the cooler northern Atlantic waters around New York and New England, only a few storms have arrived but when they do, they deliver quite a wallop as was demonstrated by The Long Island Express, the 1944 Hurricane and a relative named Carol.

CHAPTER 7

Herrrrrrrre's Carol

"She is born at sea as a speck
And starts her westward trek
Unhurriedly beginning his life
Unknowing he will cause strife
Gradually growing to become strong
Arriving where she does not belong
Along the way he gets a name
With the possibility of fame
Wind and rain bring out the fear
Destruction to what we hold dear
Anticipation causes the strain
And we respect the hurricane."

"Hurricane"
LOWELL BERGERON

During the last full week of August 1954, Hurricane Carol made her trek barely noticed, over the Atlantic as a weak tropical disturbance. The Providence Journal termed the cyclone: "Carol: a pretty name for a monster." She was the third hurricane of the year to form in the warm latitudes of the Atlantic, the paper noted in its post-hurricane report brochure. But by August 25, 1954, she was classified as a tropical depression as she waited, gathering strength from the warm waters in the central Bahamas. Her 70-mile-an-hour winds reclassified her to hurricane status on August 29th and she began to move slowly north. She was not the first tropical nightmare to reach the New England coast with the name Carol. Less than a year earlier on September 7, 1953, Hurricane Carol Number One made landfall in Eastport, Maine and she did considerable damage to that area, Canada and Nova Scotia, according to Sarah Bishop Valentine in her technical paper housed at the Westport Historical Society entitled "Hurricanes in New England 1635-1996." But it was Carol Number Two nine months later that made her real feelings felt in southern New England.

Television was a fairly new invention in 1954, but you could purchase a new all-electronic color set from RCA for $1,000 to watch "I Love Lucy" or even "American Bandstand" after school. For most families in Westport at the time, television was available on a black and white screen and provided frequent opportunities to view the test pattern before the broadcasting day began at seven o'clock each morning. The broadcast day usually concluded before midnight. One of the top shows at the time was "Father Knows Best," but it could only be seen on televisions in Westport that had roof top antennae. Rosemary Clooney, George Clooney's aunt, was singing "Hey There" and *Sports Illustrated* first copy hit the newsstands. New homes sold for an average of $10,250. A new car was $1,700 and gas at the pumps at both Ogden's Store in Acoaxet and Hammonds Store on Main Road in the Point was selling at 22 cents per gallon. We did not have a television set at our summerhouse on the morning that Carol hit. We did not hear Dave Garroway on the "Today Show" report that a dangerous storm was heading up the coast toward New England as he cautioned: "she's unpredictable." We did have a radio to listen to: "Amos & Andy," "The Shadow," the news and Red Sox games. They were as important to Red Sox Nation then as they are today.

WBZ radio in Boston had the strongest radio signal. Weather forecaster, Don Kent reported at 5:10 a.m. for those awake early enough to hear him that "winds veered to the southeast at Block Island and were increasing rapidly." It was not until 9:30 a.m. that the Boston Weather Bureau issued warnings to all coastal residents:

"Evacuate and seek higher ground."

In 1954, like 1938, there were no weather satellites. However, there were Naval weather radar planes like the Neptune, which flew into Carol's outer bands and within 300 feet of the churning ocean below. The plane and its crew were dragged around the eye wall until the pilots could no longer stand the terrifying experience. Carol's winds were estimated at 121 miles per hour and intensifying on August 30th, according to Charles Talcott Orloff in his book, Carol at 50: Remembering Her Fury An Historical and Pictorial History Of Hurricane Carol.

The meteorologists were in a quandary. Atmospheric conditions presented multiple scenarios as to which way this lady would turn and make landfall. The consensus by weathermen on Monday evening August 30, 1954 was that Carol would slide by Cape Cod and stay out to sea. Computer modules, now the gold standard in forecasting, had not yet been developed. However, her path up the east coast was one of the most dangerous for New England. During the night she was funneled by low pressure to the west and high pressure to the east. Her power would mimic that of the 1938 hurricane as it slammed into the southern New England coast. Sixty-foot waves raced across the waters surface as she moved over the continental shelf. She was a 20-mile-wide cyclone that would produce water between "ten and twelve feet high," according to Orloff in his digest of events surrounding the storm. "Air Force meteorologists, manning the new weather radar station at the Blue Hill Observatory, became alarmed at what they were seeing. The outer bands of Carol were just becoming visible on the radar screen and confirmed that the monstrous storm was at least 100 miles further west than had been predicted and was racing directly toward the Connecticut coast," reported Orloff.

It was 6:30 a.m. on August 31st before authorities in Massachusetts first used the word "hurricane," and it was just after 7:30 a.m. before the first hurricane advisory bulletin was issued. That timing may have given some warning to the Boston area but it was almost too late for those in Westport, nearly 75 miles south on the south facing coast, situated on the right quadrant and about to get blasted. She had dead aim on the local bays - Narragansett and Buzzards. Sandwiched between the two bays is Westport.

When my Dad called long-time native Steve Howland on the phone around nine in the morning, Steve said we were safe in our house as long as the wind did not shift. But the wind did shift to the south - southeast and that is when all hell broke loose. The wind swept in off the ocean and the rain stampeded behind it. Battleship gray waves crashed onto shore, gutted and moved homes that had been built anew after the '38 hurricane and made matchsticks out of some of the structures. Vicious winds uprooted trees and snapped telephone poles as the rain came down horizontally. The white foam ocean jumped the barrier-beach roads and united with abutting ponds. Rivers exploded their banks and took boats, docks and boathouses with them. Carol arrived "at express train speed and departed as fast," reported, by the Providence Journal.

Prior to the storm reaching full strength office girl Janet Branch, clad in a bright yellow rubber rain slicker and matching hat, reached the office at the Elephant Rock Beach Club Pavilion. Janet left her home along the riverside to retrieve the "log entry book," which she took back home sensing major trouble was brewing. The ocean was popping like boiling water. The incessant noise from the surf was deafening. The wind was screaming and the salty ocean smell permeated the area for miles. Janet made it to the Elephant Rock Beach Club office and back home in record time as the thrust of the storm was biting at her heels like a mongrel wanting it's dinner.

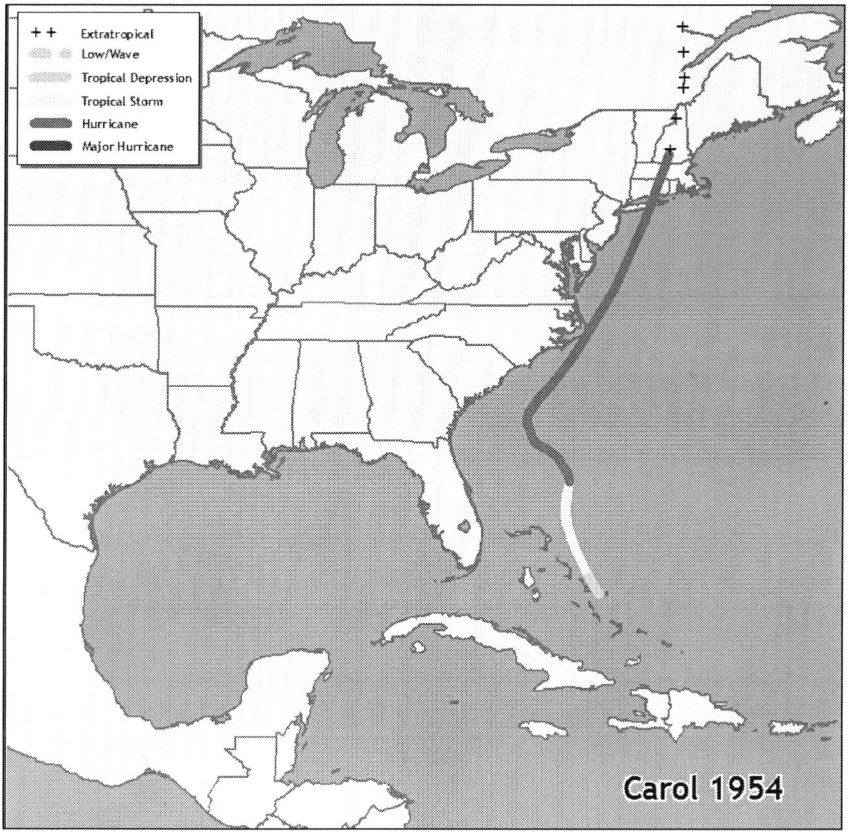

(Tracking map courtesy of NOAA)

CHAPTER 8

Hold On

"Lord of the Winds! I feel better nigh
I know thy breath in the burning sky!
And I wait, with a thrill in every vein,
For the coming of the hurricane."

"Hurricane"
W.C. Bryant

When we awoke at approximately 7:30 a.m. on August 31, 1954, the rain was mesmerizing. It fell hard on the roof of our small cottage. The cottage was only 900 square feet with five rooms, two of which were bedrooms and a tiny loo with a bathtub. The absence of a shower was typical of the homes that were built at that time. There was a slightly larger-than-galley-type kitchen, a great room and dining area that were bisected by a red brick fireplace with a contrasting tan brick mantle. An attached one stall garage would, years later, be transformed into a third bedroom. Since this was our first full year of ownership, most of the natural oak furniture was still "early Steve Howland" or better yet, "early Westport Harbor." The farmer, land baron and property owner, sold my parents his fully furnished ocean-view bungalow, which he had rented for a number of prior seasons. All the homes and land were located in his 1950 Approved Subdivision, which stretched from the Acoaxet Club southerly along the east side of Howland Road to Atlantic Avenue.

Howland had built and fully furnished our home as a "spec" house and rented it to others for a few years before my Dad purchased it from him in October 1953 for $9,900. Howland had contracted with Raymond Bixby from Little Compton to build two more spec houses to our west near the large rock on Hillside Road. They are still standing today, as is the rock.

Our house came complete with earwigs, spiders and gnats. The earwigs, some the size of aircraft carriers, seemed to live in the bathroom because the ugly little creatures with the pincers (forceps) loved damp conditions. The spiders also thrived at our house and never seemed to be dissuaded from a long-term vacation at the beach regardless of how they were treated. As large as some earwigs were, gnats were the opposite. They showed up exclusively at night and were attracted to light. Many homes installed yellow, outside porch lights, which falsely promised to not attract the annoying critters. If an outside light – regardless of the color - was left on at night, they swarmed around and buzzed like crazy but unlike mosquitoes they never bit. Some were so small that if a window was left open for the benefits of a cool summer breeze (no air conditioning at beach homes at that time) and the interior lights were left on they'd penetrate through the tightest screens toward that beacon. After turning in for the night my parents would lock the doors (the only time of day they were locked at our house or any other beach house) and often they left on a bathroom light. That is when the earwigs and gnats really partied and coated the walls and floors. The gnats were dead on the partitions, in the sink and all over the floor by morning light but the earwigs' rate of survival was much longer.

It was a typical summer place with an east-facing porch on a 9,800 square-foot lot swept by wonderful sea breezes complemented by the roar of the ocean and the smell of the salt water, which generally was very aromatic. On August 31, 1954, the ocean breeze would turn into a screeching wind and the salt-water spray would coat the windows, thereby curtailing visibility entirely. The smell of the kelp from the churning ocean floor would permeate the air with a pungent stench of rotten eggs.

"Not to worry," said my Dad on August 31, 1954 as he went about his normal early morning vacation rituals. He sat down at the dining room table with his bow tie and sport coat and settled in for a breakfast of honeydew melon, orange juice, and toast with honey from the comb and a cup of high-test coffee served by his wife.

Since my Mother did not work outside the home which was common then, she devoted herself to our care and comfort, which included preparing and serving the meals, cleaning the house, hand-washing the dishes and using a wooden board with a small tin, grooved surface made by Columbus Washboard Co. for washing clothes like socks and underwear. Their ad noted that it was "ideal for silks, hosiery and lingerie or handkerchiefs: just the right size to fit in a bucket, pail or lavatory… packs easily into a suitcase or traveling bag." Items like sheets and towels were sent to the commercial laundry along with shirts and pants and suits.

Next to my Dad's right hand on the table was his ever-present fly swatter, ready at a moment's notice to ward off those pesky end of season flies that had snuck in between the opening and closing of the screen doors on both the east and west side of the house.

"Come on, Champ, try this melon, you will love it," he said to me. When I demurred, as I often did at his food suggestions, he would invariably say, "You just don't know what is good." He was correct. It took years to figure it out.

He was nearing the end of his month-long vacation. Labor Day would signal that, and a little rain and wind would not ruin the month for which he waited all year. He took his vacation in August in order to be able to attend and officiate at the annual Newport Casino Men's Invitational Tennis Tournament. The grass court event attracted the best players in the world, all amateurs at the time, and Dad loved to watch Rod Laver, Roy Emerson, Ken Rosewall and

Pancho Gonzales among others, all future members of the Tennis Hall of Fame. He volunteered as a linesman and chair umpire while my mother would take an afternoon nap in the shade under the west grandstand at center court.

The weather was perfect after the first few wet days of the tournament, which ran from August 9-15 in 1954. Ham Richardson won the singles title and Hall of Famer, Australian great, Neale Frazer and his partner, Rex Hartwig, were crowned doubles champions. It was the same year that the Tennis Hall of Fame and Museum was formed. It was also less than six weeks after a milkshake-mixer salesman named Ray Kroc convinced the two McDonald brothers in Southern California to allow him to represent them as their agent to franchise their fast food restaurants. They sold hamburgers for fifteen cents and French fries and milk shakes under the golden arches.

After breakfast, as the winds picked up and the rain sounded as if it would explode through the roof into our open-beamed summer cottage, my Mother and I expressed more concern. Breakfast was prepared in a very basic kitchen by my mother. There was no microwave, no electric coffee pot, no dishwasher (she served in that capacity). The kitchen was also without a washing machine or clothes dryer. Her cooking skills were Irish/English: meat, potatoes and peas were the staple. She was also credited within the family years later with certain specific cooking instructions being added to boxes of frozen food after she inserted the entire box into the stove without first removing the outer carton.

"It does not say you need to take the cardboard on the outside of the box off prior to cooking. I've always done it this way," she said one night. She was right. It did not say that anywhere on the box until the mid 1970s. Today, frozen food box instructions all say to remove contents from the outer box before placing into the microwave or oven. Thank you, Angela.

It was time to reassess how long we might stay put. Dad turned on the radio to find out how long the storm might last. As we listened for weather updates, we discovered later that Dave Garroway spoke about Carol with his coat hanger microphone looped around his neck, but he had no more of an idea what may happen or which direction it may take than his sidekick, 52–year-old J. Fred Muggs - the chimpanzee. He concluded the broadcast with his customary saying and sign, "Peace," but it was anything but peaceful in Westport Harbor at 9 a.m. on August 31, 1954.

The closest thing we had to a meteorologist was Steve Howland, who had lived in Westport Harbor all his 78 years and had seen many a storm come and go including the "Long Island Express." He was not sure what was going on, although the barometric pressure was dropping (it got to 957 millibars), and as long as the wind stayed in its present direction, he said we had nothing to worry about.

"Fine," said Dad. "Let's have a game of cribbage."

By the time I was nine years old I was a veteran crib player. Early that morning, however, it was difficult for me to concentrate during the game on which cards to discard because the rain grew stronger, the winds picked up and howled and our shell of a house began to shake. The noise of the ocean became an incessant roar like an out-of-control freight train. Little did we know that Carol had already struck land in nearby Connecticut!

The leaks began. First in the dining area: "Quick, get a pan," said Angela. Then in the living room: "Get towels." Next it came down the face of the fireplace. At first a trickle, then it became a stream. It was a river waiting to happen.

Westport remained on the eastside of the eye of the storm at landfall as the storm raced up Narragansett Bay. The east quadrant is the most dangerous side of a hurricane. The damaging eastern eye wall of the cyclone slammed into Block Island, Rhode Island, with gusts reaching 135 miles per hour, which were the strongest ever recorded to that date.

Carol was similar to the Great New England Hurricane of 1938. Storm surge values were recorded at over 14 feet in Narragansett Bay and New Bedford Harbor. In the Bay, the depth was higher than GH38. Tides increased just before landfall in 1938 but since Carol arrived before high tide, the resulting storm tide was less. In Westport, high tide at the Point was estimated between 10:45 a.m. and 11:15 a.m. and by then the storm's first blast and the eye had raced past. It was the second half of the storm at near high tide that did most of the damage.

There is agreement that the eye wall is the deadliest part of the cyclone as it can produce the highest wind speeds and serves as an energy source for other parts of the hurricane as it shoots warm air up, causing heavy winds and rain. Both hurricanes were category 3 but the personal property devastation in Westport in 1938 was greater, with so many homes built and still standing on the beach at that time. A category three on the Saffir-Simpson Hurricane Scale of one to five produces sustained winds at landfall between 111-130 miles per hour. Extensive damage results include structural damage to homes and buildings. Trees snap and uproot and block roads along with power outages, which last for days and weeks. That is exactly what occurred during the hurricanes of 1938, 1944 and 1954.

My mother knew it was time to move. She had had enough. She said clearly and forcefully: "We're getting out of here!"

My father made a final phone call to the McDuff family to warn them. They were staying on the opposite side of the Harbor from where our house was located in a quirky cottage at Atlantic Avenue and Acoaxet Roads. Dad picked up the black rotary dial phone - no push buttons or colored versions in 1954 and certainly cell phones were not yet contemplated - and rang-up the local call with the help of the operator. Yes, operator! The town operators were located at the central office in south Westport on Horseneck Road. There was still no direct dial in Westport at that time. It took Henry McDuff some time to answer the two quick rings of the phone's party line. Many homes had party lines while some others had private lines, which were more expensive. There could have been up to four parties sharing one line with different rings. Unfortunately, when you picked up to dial out, you had to listen to make sure the line was not being used. There was always a great temptation to listen in as well, like taking a quick peek through the Elephant Rock bathhouse knotholes. It took some time and multiple rings for Henry to finally answer. My father did not realize that the McDuffs had entertained overnight visitors and all had partied a bit too long, too hard and too late into the night in true Westport Harbor fashion, giving support to the first part of the saying: The Harbor Drinks and The Point Thinks.

"Better get out, Henry. There is a major storm approaching and you are at a low level over there," he said.

No one realized at that time how low a level it was.

It was one of the last phone calls made through the MERcury exchange (636) central office that day as power and phone lines were being disrupted rapidly.

Off we went into the sheets of rain that were being driven sideway. "Hold on to each other!" Angela demanded.

It was approximately 9:30 a.m.

As we vacated our house, we spotted our neighbors to the north, Ray and Musette Smith, driving toward us in a southerly direction on Hillside Road. We were holding on to each other in the front yard heading to our black 1952 Chrysler New Yorker Coupe when my Dad flagged them down.

"Where are you going, Ray?" he screeched over the howling wind. Smith said he was going back to his "winter house" in Fall River. My father, now showing the concern he attempted to mask while he was in the house, shouted, "You'll never make it, too many trees and wires will be down. Let's all go to high ground at the Acoaxet Club where we will be safe." The Smiths agreed. We piled into the Smiths' car and turned around to head back north on Hillside Road toward the Smiths' house, which they had purchased less than four months earlier.

At that point the south-facing overhang roof on Smiths' front porch ripped loose and became air-born, sailing like a Frisbee and heading directly for the Smiths' automobile. Ray hit the brakes, not knowing where the roof would land. The roof overhang landed five feet in front of the car in the middle of the road. Just a second later and the five of us would have been killed, as the roof would certainly have crushed the car despite the fact that cars made at that time looked like and were built like tanks. Quickly, we did another about-face. Mr. Smith made a three-point turn back south on Hillside Road to Howland Road and then headed north to the Acoaxet Club.

To our left, as we exited Hillside Road onto Howland Road, we spotted an automobile parked, sheltered from the wind on the grass on the backside of the Rodgers' house. It was their family car strategically placed out of the wind so that the four children including three–week-old Christine might escape through the bathroom window into the waiting auto. Prior to that evacuation, the oldest child, teenager Geraldine, had tried to go out the rear side north - facing door, only to have the east wind rip the door off its hinges. Mr. Rodgers then went to plan B. After everyone was safely in the car they headed a mile and a half up the road to Cross Road and found shelter with Everett Coggeshall. Everett was a retired plumber. He was also the first Westport policeman, volunteer fireman, and he could also marry you in a pinch.

At about that time, the Acoaxet Club was attracting others who lived in the low-lying areas. Upon entering the clubhouse, everyone was greeted by the perennial August summer guests, the Randall Durfees. The 57–year-old Randall had his roots in Fall River and enjoyed returning yearly to rent a room at the Acoaxet Club with his wife, Inez, who at one point served as his nurse during a period of ill health. Randall was a small, slight man and Inez, his English wife, was a larger woman who had a voice like Ethel Merman. She was a take-charge person: "Stay away from the dining room windows, they may blow in!" She was intimidating to a nine-year-old but they were both kind and delightful people. They basically kept the Acoaxet Club clubhouse and dining room in business for years by renting a room for the full month of August, concluding on Labor Day.

Inez and Randall Durfee in 1958
(Photo courtesy of Ursula and C.Bennett Brown)

On the morning of August 31, 1954, Randall served as "official pourer." A sanctioned Red Cross shelter would never permit anyone to be a pourer, as Randall was on that day, but each shaken and cold person to enter the clubhouse received a shot of bourbon from Randall's own personal stock. He retrieved the bottle from room two on the second floor, which he and Inez called home. Even a certain nine–year-old redhead needed to calm down and warm up and was encouraged to accept a shot- a spot of "tea"- for medicinal purposes only.

Upon entering the clubhouse through the front door of the former farmhouse, there was a winding staircase to four guest rooms on the second floor. Room one had a private bath but was less desirable than room two which shared the bath in the hall. Room one overlooked the parking area next to the kitchen door and provided no view except to the second hole green on the golf course. Room two overlooked the two clay tennis courts and a view down the ninth hole out to the ocean. Room three was the smallest but faced the water to the south and had an adjacent bath that was also available to other houseguests. Room four had a private half–bath and a water view but the bedroom was above the noisy kitchen. There were three small rooms on the third floor accessible from a steep stairway between the second floor and a small landing above. The guests or summer staff in the three rooms with the slanted ceilings on the top level shared a small half-bath. The main floor where hurricane refugees' gathered - club membership was not a requirement that day to gain entrance - included a large L-shaped living room with two fireplaces and a number of upholstered couches and wing back chairs. Many would call the furniture "old" but club members referred to them as antiques. Perhaps New England Yankee thrift would best describe the décor of the day. Another smaller reading room was similarly decorated but also included a desk to write postcards purchased at Ogden's Store.

While Randall was pouring and Inez's voice was booming, there was a near-disaster mounting less than a half-mile away on Atlantic Avenue. The club refugees knew things were bad with the arrival of every additional entrant. The Hindleys- Mary Lou and her children, Judith, 13 years old, Charlie, age 8, Nancy, age 5, and 2– year-old Barbara, drove to the safety of the Acoaxet Club in the Hindleys' open convertible, dodging falling wires and tree limbs in the less than half-mile trek to the north. Jud Hindley and his plant foreman and summer neighbor, Ray Davis, had left early that morning to head for the family manufacturing plant in Cumberland, Rhode Island, but his convertible would be used to shuttle others to safety, including Howland Foster and his mother, Mildred. Father Stuart Foster was back working in Connecticut. Ray Davis' wife, Alice, affectionately called Magee by her husband, and young children, Ray

Howland water tower nearly destroys the Ray Davis home.
(Photo courtesy of Holly Field Sirois)

and Kathy, also took refuge at the Hindley house and eventually at the Acoaxet Club. While at the Hindleys, the Davis clan watched the water tower next to their house fall, just missing it by a few feet.

Mrs. D'Angelo, whose house on the beach would be gutted, joined other neighbors gathered on the high point of Acoaxet land. She gained a sense of personal security by seeing the crowd at the clubhouse.

Mrs. Chung, an elderly lady who wore traditional white Korean kimono attire all summer, arrived at the Acoaxet clubhouse with the Hindleys. When that group arrived, all who were in attendance were informed about beachfront homes that were being washed away. Dr. Tony D'Angelo's house next door on the west of the Rhee house, home of Mrs. Chung, on the south side of Atlantic Avenue, had become a shell. These stories and more filtered into the clubhouse with

D'Angelo's beach house in "The Harbor" after Carol.
(Photo courtesy of Lorna Phan and Holly Bronhard from the Dr. Tony D'Angelo collection)

every new arrival.Charlotte Gallery, the doctor's wife, staggered into the building wet from head to toe. She had driven herself from their beachfront home none too soon, as it later ended up in the pond on the shore of the golf course.

Mrs. Gallery was in shock. She nearly waited too long before evacuating and almost did not make it to safety. Like Red Sox star Ted Williams waiting at the plate for Indians fastball pitcher Bob Lemon to throw a little white ball at his head 90 miles per hour, Charlotte had to decide in a split second when to bail out. In her case, it was not out of the batters' box but out of what should have been the safety and comfort of her home.

Years later her long time friends, Doctor Harry and his wife, Helen Powers, confessed that she was traumatized by the experience and she had vowed never again to build on the beach. Charlotte kept that vow. The Gallery's did not build on the beach again.

According to psychologists there are two types of victims in a natural disaster: direct and indirect. Direct victims like Mrs. Gallery experience an increase in anxiety such as a fear of another disaster, depression or even rage. The symptoms can manifest themselves by a schizophrenic stare, irritability or guilt. Indirect victims often ask themselves why they escaped while others did not. There is a significant mental strain for those who have experienced a disaster - it seems they need to relate their stories to others who will listen. They need to vent. When they do vent, often their memory plays tricks on them and there are exaggerations of actual events, according to some psychologists.

The remains of the Gallery home in the pond.
(Photo courtesy of Lorna Phan and Holly Bronhard from the Dr. Tony D'Angelo collection)

Not everyone on the Howland side of Westport Harbor ended up at the club. As was noted, the Rodgers family sough refuge at Coggeshall house on Cross Road. The Hanson family took a different route. Doctor Al Hanson left for work as an optometrist in Attleboro early that morning accompanied by his mother-in-law. He left behind his wife, Mim, and children Wendy, David and Susie. They lived diagonally across the street from the Hindley house and in close proximity to the 67-acre Richmod Pond. The pond was to the west of Howland Road and to the east of Brayton Point which straddles the Rhode Island state line and is the most westerly section of Westport. Although their house was to the east of the pond, the possibility of flooding made evacuation a good idea.

With the weather rapidly deteriorating, Mim Hanson ushered her children into her car and headed to her cousin's home in Little Compton about 10 miles inland to the west. She avoided fallen tree limbs and wires and reached his house near the Town Commons in time to watch the steeple on the Congregational Church fall. When they made it back home after the storm, Dr. Al returned to find his family safe and sound. The next day his daughter, Wendy, went exploring and found their Elephant Rock bathhouse locker on the golf course fairway, bathing suits and towels still hung on the dowels drying and ready to use.

CHAPTER 9

The Bus

Simultaneous to my parents and I and the Smiths leaving for higher and safer ground, the Cozy Cab bus was departing the bus terminal behind the Granite Block in downtown Fall River for its morning round trip to Westport Harbor. Those on board had no inkling that this trip might be the last for the bus numbered 54 in the fleet. Thirty-year-old Jimmy Graham, son of the owner, was the driver, as he had been for the past eight years.

Jimmy was a slight man with short-cropped, receding light hair. His father and Al Tremblay, his father's partner, owned The Cozy Cab Bus Company, which included a number of taxicabs as well as a few buses. When he departed the Fall River terminal, he had four passengers on board the bus for his trip down Stafford and Crandall Roads in Tiverton, Rhode Island, to Westport Harbor, including 18-year-old Mary McGowan from Somerset. Her mother had driven Mary to the bus terminal and the teenager was heading back from a day off to her six–day-a-week job as a nanny in Acoaxet.

Cozy Cab bus driver Jimmy Graham (Photo courtesy of The Herald News)

"It was raining and blowing quite hard, nobody was worried, though. The weather report had only said winds up to fifty miles an hour with gusts to seventy," according to Mary.

By the time Mary and Jimmy reached Ogden's Store in Acoaxet, the trip had become increasingly difficult. Tree limbs were down along River Road in Westport and boats had come off their moorings and were cruising unmanned up the river. The salt spray attacking the bus from the river had gotten worse the farther south they traveled into the Acoaxet area. It was a bit past 10 a.m. at that time. Other passengers had disembarked on their way from Fall River at their designated stops in Tiverton. Mary was still not concerned; after all, she was just a few days short of her 19th birthday and had no fear at all.

My parents and me and Mr. and Mrs. Smith arrived at the Acoaxet Club around 9:45 a.m. about 45 minutes before high tide and approximately 15 minutes before the blue and white, medium-size bus arrived at Ogden's. Mary needed to stay on the bus until she reached Peckham Lane, north of the Acoaxet Club on Howland Road. She would need to ride the bus along Atlantic Avenue with Jimmy and a new passenger, teenager, Dana Plante, who worked at the store/inn during the summer months.

After the 10 minute pit stop at the store it was time to get back on the road; Mr. Graham to finish his route, Dana to enjoy a day off and Mary to get to the home of Doctor and Mrs. Burton Bryan to babysit for the four children including the one-month old Robbie. No one on the bus contemplated not going forward or at least did not say so openly, and when the bus approached the bathhouses of Elephant Rock Beach Club on Atlantic Avenue, it was obvious that the water had breached the land and had gone over the road. Atlantic Avenue is the road bisecting the ocean on the south and Cockeast Pond to the north.

"Jimmy didn't think it was too much," Mary remembers over 55 years later.

While the bus driver and his passengers studied the situation on Atlantic Avenue, the occupants of the house to the north were watching them. The Snow family lived at the corner of Atlantic Avenue and Remington Road to the east of, and about six feet above, the Elephant Rock Beach Club parking lot. Borden Snow, who was 12 at the time, recalls watching with his older brother, Brad, his younger sister, Julie and their mother, Flossie. (Their dad, Bill, was back up in Dedham, Massachussetts working.)

"We could hear the bus coming. It stopped. Jimmy surveyed the situation ahead. Then the engine started revving. We looked at each other with disbelief. He wasn't going to try to cross that stretch of road with the ocean roaring, waves breaking on the road and obvious disaster waiting, was he? Yes, he was, and off he went." recounted Borden. "Jimmy and whoever was in that bus were literally taking their lives in their hands. We watched as it moved, splashing across Atlantic Avenue until it came to an abrupt halt. For us kids this was exciting stuff," recalled Snow.

The water got deeper as the bus proceeded along Atlantic Avenue, and at about the halfway mark the engine stalled and would not restart. After waiting in the bus with the water and waves crashing on its south-facing side, the three musketeers abandoned ship, which now was being moved in a northerly direction by the storm. If they stayed in the bus they were in danger and if they left the bus there was peril certainly waiting. It was approaching high tide but those on board the bus were neither aware of that nor would they have cared.

They decided to evacuate. Mary and Dana removed their shoes and put them in their raincoat pockets. The driver took his coin changer, which held the proceeds from the day's trip. The churning water was nearly hip deep when they disembarked from the bus. The water tore Mary's socks off as soon as she touched it. They looked hurriedly for the nearest safe house. It was Bill and Flossie Snows' next to the Elephant Rock Pavilion, but once they went past the shelter of the bus, they realized they could never make it back there. The waves were too strong. They headed north to the dock on the pond. It was getting close to 10:30 a.m. and shortly thereafter, the eye of the hurricane passed over, merely an hour before high tide. It had all come together to create the perfect storm on Atlantic Avenue, the three-quarter mile stretch that connects the two sides of Westport Harbor.

Boom! The first wave hit.

The blue and white painted bus slid sideways. Then a series of left jabs and right hooks slapped the south facing side of the bus.

Boom!

Boom!

The bus tipped over on its side and was knocked right off the road. It eventually floated out into the pond where it remained upright for days until it was salvaged.

The pond was and still is the home to a beginners' sailing program and "pond boats" are used to teach local youngsters the basics of sailing. Individual families owned their pond boats at that time; today, the Spindle Rock Club owns them. There were as many as a dozen pond boats moored or tied up at the small dock on the south side of the pond. In the middle of the pond was Gull Rock, a spot that young sailors stopped to visit as they cruised the snapping turtle-infested waters. The depth of the pond was generally shallow, not

Submerged Cozy Cab Bus in Cockeast Pond in the Harbor
(Photo courtesy of The Herald News)

over a child's head until you reached the northern most boundaries. It is about a quarter mile wide and nearly three quarter miles long.

The section of the shoreline of the pond on the west runs along the golf course fairways of the Acoaxet Club. On the east side there is an opening to the west branch of the Westport River called the herring run that allows for the flow of salt water from the river into the spring-fed fresh water pond. On the north there were two homes and along the southern border sat the Atlantic Ocean just waiting to erupt.

With devastation all around them, the bus occupants reached the pond boat dock. By this time Mary had lost her brother's raincoat and her own blazer, but she had put her wallet into her pants pocket. As all three tried to decide what to do, she watched houses torn from their foundations move past them up the pond.

"The water was rising and the wind and waves were getting stronger. Suddenly, something hit my head," Mary recalls. It was a part of the small dock that was breaking up. Dana and Mary found an overturned pond boat and held on. As the wind pushed both the ocean and the pond water northerly, the waves rushed over the boat and Mary and the Plante boy thought they would lose their grip and their hands would be torn off the boat. Mary's billfold was gone but Dana still had his coat on and his shoes were still in his pocket. The first land sighting for the two was the golf course and "that was the first time I thought we would survive," said Mary. But then things stalled. The golf course was fading away. They were heading dead north toward the Pelton house, almost three quarters of a mile away from the dock. Mary, then a student at Bridgewater College, and the younger Dana, still holding tight to their pond boat, began to move northerly. The waves rushed over their heads as they headed up the pond. Muskrats crawled over them, holding onto their hair and heads like a life raft, in desperate attempts to survive.

The muskrats did the same to Jimmy who would eventually find his way to the kitchen door of the Acoaxet clubhouse. Jimmy held tight to an upside-down rowboat as he, too, floated in the pond. He was heading to the west side of the pond toward the Acoaxet Club property. Jimmy later said he was heading toward "the island" (Gull Rock) but was swept past it. When he was about to abandon hope of survival, he was hurled toward the golf club shoreline to eventually reach land at the green on fifth hole, which ended up being submerged.

"I looked like Robinson Crusoe," he told a local newspaper reporter when asked about his harrowing experience. After walking nearly 500 yards up the second golf hole fairway, he reached the Acoaxet Club clubhouse. He banged on the locked kitchen door around noon, which was after the eye passed. I was in the kitchen at the time, so I opened the door to see Jimmy, eyes like saucers, in shock, looking like a wet rat himself.

While Graham was being wrapped in a blanket and given Randall's top shelf liquor, no doubt he needed more than a shot; the teenagers were still missing. Jimmy related the entire story and how he had last seen his passengers at the dock. Word went from the clubhouse to Ed Phinney. Phinney sent his crew to look for the teens. One of the search party members was Dale Plante, Dana's twin. He spent summers working at the Acoaxet Club. Dale set out walking down the fifth hole to the pond to find survivors - he was unaware until the following day that his twin brother had been on the bus.

Earlier that morning, Alice Tripp, who lived about a mile inland at Bojuma Farm came knocking at the Pelton's door to warn Mrs. Pelton and her two teenage children, who were new to the area, of the very bad storm that was approaching. Alice had first-hand experience of the power of the wind and sea. Her family, the Dennetts, owned a home just north of the Elephant Rock Pavilion before GH38, which was destroyed completely. Alice had also witnessed the effects of the 1944 hurricane and knew that the Pelton home, despite being over three quarters of a mile from the ocean but on the banks of Cockeast Pond, could easily be subject to the water surge and be flooded out. Mr. Pelton was back in Connecticut at work. Mrs. Pelton dispatched the children, Lee and her brother, Harry, "down to the harbor to get our little boats out of the water," recalled Lee. When they reached the river, they found the boats had been removed and they quickly did an about - face to get home just before the road washed out near the herring run. The Cozy Cab bus had already passed by this section of River Road. A bit after Lee and Harry returned home, Mrs. Pelton was too worried and upset to stay in the house. Everyone moved to higher ground and found refuge at the Damon home on Peckham Lane with Mrs. Damon who was alone at the time. Mr. Damon, like most men who were not on vacation, was working in Boston during the week while his family stayed in

Westport. The Damons lived across the road from the Bryan house, which was Mary McGowan's original destination. The Pelton house was almost at sea level and the storm deposited wreckage within five feet of the house. Mary and Dana were forced to stay on the boat, waves breaking over them and being pushed into land where they then could move forward. They came to rest below the Pelton house and made their way through the heavy brush and briars to the front door of the home. When they got to land, they separated but reconnected moments before finding a sanctuary at Peltons. After forcing their way into the house, they wrapped themselves in blankets and were eventually found by the search party. They were then brought to the club to be reunited with Jimmy, wrapped in more blankets from the inventory of Miss Coggeshall (no relation to Everett), the clubhouse manager, and to be warmed by a shot or two of Randall's most coveted beverage. No one informed twin brother, Dale, who was still out on the golf course looking for survivors, that they had been found and were safe in one of the clubhouse guest rooms. It was many hours later before he finally learned of his brother's fate.

When the Peltons returned home, they knew someone had been in the house but did not know whom until a few days later when the story of the survivors of the bus incident became known. But even then as there is today there was confusion as to who was on the bus with the driver.

"It is miraculous that we are still alive," Graham told a reporter for The Herald News a few days later.

CHAPTER 10

Miz Ma'amselle

The Shaw children and their mother, Ruth, made it to high ground at the Hindleys house, after a brief intermediate stop, to wait out the storm. Children Dick, Nancy, Judy and cousin, Rhoda, who was spending the summer with them, followed Ruth's orders. Their dad, Frank, had returned on Sunday evening to work in Connecticut.

Earlier in the morning, Dick and Nancy had gone for a walk on Elephant Rock Beach to see what treasures the rough surf had deposited. Finding nothing of consequence and being buffeted by the increasingly strong gale winds, they returned home to their ocean-front cottage, which always seemed to be a work in progress. In fact, in 1954, their Dad had been working on the house all summer, building a new fireplace that never experienced a flame nor did smoke pass up the flue. This was not the first Shaw family house on the beach. The Great Hurricane of 1938 demolished the original cottage built by their great-grandfather Pease from Fall River. Now, Hurricane Carol was bearing down on the family again.

"When we returned, having been blown along the beach but finding nothing of interest, the fierce wind blew the screen door off its hinges right out of Dick's hand, which really upset Mom," according to Nancy Shaw May. "Ironically, it turned out that the screen door was the only part of the house we recovered insurance on, as it was determined to be wind damage," related Nancy.

The Shaws thought it best to go to higher ground, so Dick went below the prefab house that had been promoted in advertisements as "hurricane proof" and tried to unhinge it. The concept was to allow the main part of the house to float away off its pilings in bad weather and survive intact to be repositioned at a later date. In actuality, the concept worked at the Richardson house next door, which later came to rest in one piece across Atlantic Avenue. Dick Shaw, however, was unable to unbolt the hardware. That, combined with the attached fireplace, allowed a large portion, but not all, of the dwelling to float away. The Shaw house, unlike the Richardson abode, was blown up the pond near the golf course. The Richardson family eventually moved their nearly intact home up the street onto higher ground at the top of Hillside Road on a lot owned by Steve Howland.

As the tempest intensified the Shaw family left the cottage and crossed Atlantic Avenue to the Eddy house, which had the telephone service that the Shaws did not have in 1954. Mr. Shaw had called from the Nutmeg State to tell Kitty Eddy that the storm was turning into a hurricane and his family should be told to evacuate to the Eddy homestead. That message was transmitted more than over a half-hour after being received according to Dick Shaw, still frustrated over a half-century later by the slow notice to his family.

As with all storms of this magnitude the question remained: what to do with the animals? The Shaw's had a white boxer dog, Blitz, and a pet skunk. The family took themselves with the clothes on their backs and their pets in tow to Kitty Eddy's house. Kitty was the sister of Sturges Richardson from whom she bought the house in 1952 after he moved across the road and built a prefab cottage on the ocean directly next door to the Shaws place.

Kitty Eddy and her husband were at home with their three children, Bart, Martha and Susan, and their dog. After the Shaw family arrived and Mr. Eddy hammered nails into the doors to keep both the front and rear doors sealed from the storm, it was not long before rescue personnel arrived, instructing the group to go to higher ground. So, off to the Hindley house on Howland Road the parade went - all but Miz Ma'amselle, the pet skunk that was left to fend for herself on the kitchen table in the hurricane-vulnerable Eddy house on Atlantic Avenue. The group exited through a bathroom window since the doors had been nailed shut. They cut the clothesline and tied each other together and began their journey up the hill through the vacant house lots, past our cottage to what they believed to be another safe haven.

Nancy recalls the trek up to the Hindley house. "I remember our group climbing up the incline towards the Hindley house, hanging on to each other in a human chain and struggling against the wind, which we later learned reached 125 miles per hour. The Hindley's side door opened off a breezeway between their ranch design house and the garage. The first among us to reach it was my brother, Dick, who was whipped by the wind right past the door on the slick, painted concrete, and deposited on the driveway on the other side. After that, someone stood in the open doorway and caught each of us as we went sailing past," Nancy related.

On the side of the structure opposite the main section of the house was the one car garage connected by the breezeway. Mary-Lou Hindley had dispatched oldest child, Judith, to the automobile to listen for weather reports on the car radio. Not only was power being disrupted in this coastline community but also radio transmission signals were poor at best. Car radios provided the best source of information. Unfortunately, none of the Providence radio stations disseminated any weather information that morning while Judith was listening, but weather report or no, the concern of the group took over and shuttle rides began to the Acoaxet Club which was on even higher ground.

"The aftermath was surreal.... the waves and destruction are still etched in my mind," Judith recalled in 2010.

After settling in with the crowd at the Hindleys', the Shaw family heard that elderly Maria Chung and her dog were believed to be still in her beach house. Seventeen-year-old Dick Shaw went to her rescue since it was rumored that her family had gone off that day early in the morning and she had been left alone in the house. Dail Rhee, Mrs. Chung's grandson, and Dick Shaw were close friends. Dick set off on his mission and found her in a second floor bedroom as the waves rushed through the south side of the main floor of the house and out the north side. Also in the house was the family pet, Wou-Wou, a collie so named by Vonnie Rhee, Mrs. Chung's daughter-in-law.

Nancy Shaw May related: "Mrs. Chung spoke only Korean, and Dick had a hard time convincing her to leave the house with him. Fortunately, she was a tiny woman, because he wound up carrying her. Apparently she didn't want to get her feet wet!"

"I realized at the Hindley house that no one was at home at the Rhee house except Dail's grandmother," related Dick. As the first half of the storm was raging, Dick set off on his own, back down to the oceanfront, to find Mrs. Chung. "When I reached the two-story beach front house which was protected by a three-foot-high and two-foot-wide fortress-like concrete barrier sea wall along the ocean side, the water was lapping the wall and sloshing up onto the first floor windows and had just started to break through into the first level," related Shaw. (Future owners of the house added to the wall, making it four feet high and three feet wide, which today provides some degree of comfort - no matter how small - to the present owners.)

"I went inside and found my way up the narrow stairs all the while calling, Mrs. Rhee, Mrs. Rhee, but there was no answer. I believed that to be her name as she was Dail's grandmother, but it was years later that I learned her name was Mrs. Chung," * related Shaw.

*In Korea a woman retains her maiden name even after marriage.

When he finally found her in the back bedroom, it was difficult for young Shaw to communicate with the elderly non–English –speaking woman. He eventually had to carry her from her bedroom to the Hindley house on the hill.

Shaw never did notice their dog, which was found unharmed the next day when young Rhee and his cousin returned to the battered home.

By now the Hindley house was overflowing and many of the occupants stood at the window, watching debris sail by, which was not a safe thing to do. The debris could have easily sailed through the window into the house, as porch chairs, tables and umbrellas can easily become airborne.

Mrs. Chung stayed in a corner, praying in Korean.

The Shaws watched from the Hindley picture window that faced east toward Cockeast Pond to see their cottage swept across the road and into the pond. There it collapsed.

Rescue workers made their way to Hindleys; it was time for everyone to move again just as the sun came out. Even at this high point of land the rescue workers felt there was still danger.

The crowd at the Hindley house also watched with disbelief as the Cozy Cab bus also washed off the road into Cockeast Pond and all hoped no one was still on board.

Mrs. Shaw felt the safety of her children would be more guaranteed if they moved again to even higher ground.

According to Nancy, "She went outside again and cut down the Hindley's clothesline, tied us all together (including the dog, Blitz), and led us through Steve Howland's fields to the Howland house, then operating as a sort of hotel. There we waited out the storm."

The Shaws were not the only family to experience multiple coastal hurricanes. On West Horseneck beach the Souza family was experiencing its third hurricane in less than twenty years. In 1935, 30 year-old physician Charles Souza from Dighton, Massachusetts, who was a general practicioner at Morton Hospital in Taunton, convinced his wife, Rose, to invest in oceanfront property in Westport. In fact, it was a "shack" with no electricity, according to his daughter, Lois Souza McCormick. In 1938, the most severe hurricane of the century lashed into Westport and destroyed their summer shack. Fortunately, they, their 4 year-old son, Charlie and 2 year-old daughter, Cynthia, survived.

The Doctor and his wife decided to rebuild, add electricity and stay put. Six years later they were visited again by a ferocious storm in 1944. Again the house was destroyed and again they decide to rebuild, this time around their bathtub and refrigerator with its metal ice cube trays with levers, that had now made it, still in working order after a good cleaning through two hurricanes. By then 3–year-old Lois was part of the family. Being a thrifty family, Charlie and Rose had saved some money and hired a contractor who promised that what he would build would never be destroyed by a hurricane.

Ten more years of idyllic summers passed for the family. When Charlie and Cynthia became teenagers, they walked down the beach from the family house to jobs at nearby Gendreau's Concession Stand, previously called Hutchinson's Midway Pavilion, located in the dunes at Sixteenth Avenue and West Beach Road. Sixteenth Avenue rose 75 feet into the sand dunes and was a quarter mile long and ran north to south from John Reed Road to West Beach Road (a great road for teens to put the pedal to the metal in their cars or trucks and fly off the macadam into the air at the top of the hill.) The Souza kids also worked at Plante's Pavilion, which was also known as the Spindrift. It was the Plante family who owned the eating and drinking establishment and did so for more than 60 years. The parking lots of both establishments filled up early with beach-going traffic on weekends and both did a brisk business selling seafood and beverages to hungry day-trippers who clogged Main Road for miles.

Henry Plante was the owner in 1954 and was preceded for years by his father who rebuilt after each hurricane. Henry and his family lived year-round on the second floor and on the morning Carol hit, they got out just in time. Henry still planned to continue to operate the business after Carol. His plans changed when the State informed homeowners and businesses alike on Horseneck that the Commonwealth had other designs on that property.

Due to his occupation, Doctor Souza needed to be conscious of the weather. He heard that a storm had reached the outer banks of North Carolina on August 30, 1954, and decided to stay at his home/office in Dighton that evening after notifying his wife and three children that the remnants of the storm in the form of potentially heavy rain could be expected the next day. He was not concerned about his "hurricane proof" house but his family needed to be on the alert.

Their next-door teenage neighbor, Tony Hazen, joined the Souza siblings the following morning and like their future friends, the Shaw children on Elephant Rock Beach, they patrolled Horseneck pulling up rowboats on logs up onto higher ground into the dunes. Holding on to each other in the face of the east-blowing wind and needle-piercing sand pelting their skin, they made it home.

Rose decided it was time to vacate. She had seen the results of such storms over the years. Into their car the four piled and proceeded east along West Beach Road to 16th Avenue and then to John Reed Road toward the Point Bridge. Passing over the viaduct they could still see their 28-foot cabin cruiser named, CE–EM-ES moored at Tripp's Boat Yard. That was the last time they saw their boat in one piece, as it was found weeks later miles up–river near Great Island.

Today, Lois asserts that they were the last car over the bridge since the vehicle behind them got stuck in rising high water at the south end of the link. The Souza car followed the Hazen car as river water nipped at the floorboards. The car that did not make it may have belonged to George Smith and his wife who were the last to cross the bridge on foot. The water on Main Road by that time was knee-deep.

The Souza family navigated the eight-mile drive up Main Road weaving around down trees and wires, driving through yards to safety at Saint John the Baptist Catholic Church. They were then moved from the church and directed by local police to a shelter at town hall in order to centralize and identify survivors. It was there that Doctor Souza found his family hours later as he traveled from home, hoping his family was safe, as he knew from first-hand experience the destructive power of a hurricane upon his home site.

J. Roger Sisson had taken an atypical day off on August 31, 1954. His mother-in-law and sister-in-law owned a home on Horseneck and he elected to enjoy a day at the beach with his wife, Jackie who was eight and one half months pregnant with their son, Lincoln, and their five other children: Jay, age 8, Rick, 7, Jacqueline, 4, Christine, 3, and Gregory, 1- (tragically they had lost their 6–year – old, daughter, Paula, only months before to a tonsillectomy gone terribly wrong at a local hospital).

Mr. and Mrs. George Smith safely crossed the Point Bridge.
(Photo courtesy of The Herald News)

With all those mouths to feed, not surprisingly, Sisson held two jobs. He was co-owner with his brother, George, of a small radio station in Fall River with the call letters WALE. They were in competition with a larger, more established station, WSAR "Ahoy there matey, it's 1480" and like Avis they had to "try harder." It meant working nearly every day for 18 hours per day. J. Roger generally awoke very early to get the station on air by 5 a.m. and then moved about the area selling on-air advertising time well into each evening. As well as being one of the owners, J. Roger was an early morning on-air personality where his sister-in-law, Madeleine Hamel, also worked. He had been elected to the Great and General Court of the Commonwealth of Massachusetts as a Representative from the Eighth

The Sisson clan pre-Carol
(Photo courtesy of Madeleine Hamel)

District in Bristol County. That summer the legislature worked through the summer, a rare event, and Sisson was exhausted and in need of a day off. There was no time for formal vacations but a day off at the beach with his family at the end of summer was something to relish.

As the wind and rain shook the cottage, Madeleine who was working at the radio station in Fall River, called a Westport neighbor, one of the few who had a phone at the time. She had read of the pending storm on the early morning ticker tape. She suggested they all might want to vacate to higher ground. All seven-plus Sissons and the family dog, a german shepherd named Jigger, piled into the car that J.Roger drove down John Reed Road. They could hear the roar of the ocean biting at their heels to their south and could see the churning river and The Let to the north. The Let is a portion of the east branch of the river that culminates at East Beach Road. Soon, they had passed over the bridge and began to feel secure.

On the north side of the viaduct stood Laura's Restaurant and its next-door neighbor, the Pacquachuck Inn. As the family drove by the Inn, J. Roger had a thought: "I should call the station and do a live report from Westport Point." There were no cell phones in those days so Sisson stopped the car, ordered everyone out, except the dog, and took his family into the Inn where the owner, George Reis offered to make everyone clam chowder. Sisson used their phone to call WALE.

Once the clan was inside the Inn, the water began to climb. It rushed under the doors and began to rise within the building. J. Roger and Jackie moved the children to the second floor but could not trust their youngest, Gregory, only a year old, from crawling into the water, so they found some rope and tied him to the bed posts while J.Roger went back down stairs to use the phone:

" This is J. Roger Sisson reporting live from the Pacquachuck Inn at Westport Point," he announced to his listeners.

East Beach devastation.
(Photo courtesy of The Herald News)

All the while the water was rising. He witnessed Laura's break up and float into the river with three occupants inside. He saw the George T. Leach and Son Marine Services building float from west to east across Main Road just north of the Inn and into the river.

Water continued to rise in the first floor of the Inn, reaching the bar and the shelf where bottles of liquor were waiting to be served that night. The bottles then started to float in the water. As the liquor bottles floated by Sisson, Reis and another man would calm their nerves with a swig or two from the bottles as they bobbed past.

The water receded as quickly as the 15 minutes it took to arrive and Jackie Sisson who was admittedly frightened, demanded they leave. Everyone climbed back into the car and the Sisson tribe departed. No more on-air radio reports but J. Roger wanted to go back to see what happened to the cottage. They were not allowed to go back over what was determined to be the unsafe bridge. The Sisson family drove all the way around to the other side of town and traveled down Horseneck Road as far as they could. East Beach Road was impassable and the homes on the beach were totally gone.

The only thing left of the family house was the sand pipe. He found their refrigerator with the eggs and orange juice still intact near where his neighbor once lived three lots away. All he could do was return to his vehicle and take the long, sad drive back to their permanent residence in Somerset. Along the way, coming in the opposite direction from Fall River was a car driven by Jackie's sister, Madeleine, and her mother. Both left their places of employment in Fall River and headed to Westport to check on their family and their home. J. Roger gave them the good and bad news - the family was safe but the family beach home was gone.

CHAPTER II

After The Eye

In the midst of the chaos at the Acoaxet clubhouse that had by this time become a shelter, the sun came out. The wind stopped and the sky brightened. Unlike a tornado, where shelter can be sought in a basement and when the incredible winds have passed it is over, a hurricane has a one-two punch. The eye of Carol was 50 miles wide. The surf was still breaking with force but the sun was out and the wind had diminished.

It was around 11a.m. The wind had slowed and then picked up again until nearly 2 p.m., which was an unusually long period of time for a storm to restart and continue after the eye had passed.

Tom Rodgers broke away from Coggeshall's house during the eye of the storm. He took his eight-millimeter movie camera and headed back to his front porch at the corner of Howland Road and Atlantic Avenue to capture the devastation on film. When the storm returned with a vengeance, he retreated to his family about a mile north on Cross Road and stayed there until the storm subsided later in the day. The family then returned a few hours afterwards to find their home still in one piece except for some wind damage. It was then that Mr. Rodgers resumed filming and captured the Richardson house in the middle of Atlantic Avenue along with the destruction that occurred at other oceanfront properties.

At this time, elderly Steve Howland lived in a smaller farmhouse behind his hilltop hotel. His two farm hands, Manny Medeiros and Bud Davis, were on duty early that morning, milking the half dozen cows in preparation for Steve to make his milk, cream, eggs and veggie deliveries to the insulated milk boxes at front doors around the Harbor. As the storm intensified, Bud, who was 42 years old at the time and Manny who was older, were isolated in the dump truck down below the hill near the cow barn. The old vehicle seemed to move two feet forward and three feet in reverse as the wind intensified. Both had experienced GH38 and although they did not know what was going on with the weather during that storm, they certainly did in 1954. They had rounded up the cows that had been huddled together in the fields and brought them back to the barn, securing them in their neck harnesses. When the eye came through, it was time for the farm hands to make a break for it and head for the milk room in the shed behind the farmhouse where Steve was holed up alone. As they motored near the house, they could see that the giant maple tree to the south of the house had made an unscheduled visit into the front door, leaving Steve trapped inside. The farm hands retreated to the safety of the milk house next door and waited out the balance of the hurricane before rescuing their boss.

When Jimmy, the bus driver, arrived at the Acoaxet Clubhouse after 11a.m. he related that he had survived by holding on to an overturned pond boat until it washed up on the fifth hole of the golf course. He then trudged up nearly 500 yards up to the white-shingled clubhouse kitchen door. He appeared as if he had gone to hell and back, and his story was confirmed by the terror in his eyes and the panic in his voice. He was in shock, but was able to relate his story. He knew he had two bus passengers, a teenage boy and girl, but he and they had become separated due to the ferocity of the storm. He did not know their names but knew they often rode the bus.

Rumors quickly spread that the boy on the bus was Dail Rhee. His uncle and aunt, Dan and Vonnie Rhee, had left South Korea prior to the start of the Korean War, purchased ocean front land, and built a beach house in 1946. They had never experienced a hurricane. Dail would frequently take the bus to Adamsville to work in the general store owned by Bordie Tripp. The girl on the bus was also misidentified as Debby Morse, the sister of daredevil, David, the daughter of Ken and Helen Morse, who lived on River Road approximately one mile north of the ocean and across the road from Borden and Alice Tripp.

The driving rain was coming down sideways as the Acoaxet Club grounds crew search party headed for the pond. Dale Plante encountered a dazed Jimmy Graham as they struggled past each other in opposite directions along the shoreline of the golf course and Cockeast Pond. Dale reported years later that it felt like the soles of his sneakers were burning (in fact, the bottom front portion had been torn back to the heel as a result of the strong winds and torrential rain) as he walked about the golf course, looking for survivors. He did not realize at the time that his twin brother might be one of those bus passengers. He witnessed muskrats coming out of the water and later related that Dana thought he was "a goner' but held on to the boats and logs with the girl, Mary, whom he did not know at the time. The wind then shifted again to the east, the opposite direction from whence it first came, then things exploded and Carol returned with a vengeance.

After the eye passed and the storm resumed, the Snow family watched the waves break at about the four-foot level in the beach club parking area, which was about six feet below their home. The waves were higher than at any time they had ever seen them reaching half way up the utility poles. At various times, the beach club Pavilion would break up and rush by their windows. When the largest portion of the structure cascaded by and up into the pond, the Snow family watched it slam full force and shatter into pieces on Gull Rock. It was then that Flossie Snow took her mother, who lived next door at the time in the "Round House" and her three children, out of the house and headed onto higher ground. She had seen enough!

Eileen Sheehan was 10 years old during Carol. She and her mother, Rhoda and grandmother, Sophie Wheeler, lived in multiple houses on the 60-acre Wheeler riverside farm, which was adjacent to Ben's Point located on the west bank of the West Branch of the river. The large family home on the hill was rented for the summer and the tenants were still in the house on August 31, 1954. She and her family including younger siblings Stafford, age 8, Billy, age 7 and Marion, age 2, were therefore, occupying the Boathouse on the river's edge. Rhoda, who was six months pregnant at the time with her fourth child, Philip, had decided years before to build the boathouse as a summer place on the river for her family. Next door, only a few feet away, was grandmother Sophie who was living in the Hurricane House that abutted the Canoe House that was used primarily for storage.

The Hurricane House was so named because it was the remnants of a boathouse owned by Doctor Ralph French and, like his ocean front house both were destroyed in GH38. French never attempted to salvage anything and left the remains on the Wheeler land for their use. It was taken from the turnip field below the main house and erected on riverside land at the confluence of the channel that moves up from the West Branch of the river into the harbor and then around Bailey Flat toward Westport Point and the East Branch.

By early morning on the day Carol arrived, the Sheehan family watched the river and ocean to the south explode. They could not separate the sea from the sky, as everything was pitch black. It was that same blackness that Wayne Branch would describe as he left his riverfront home. Wind gusts caused the walls in the Boathouse to shake. Rhoda instructed the three older children to lean onto the walls to support them upright. The water was rising. It was time to move the children next door with Sophie into the Hurricane House on higher ground. But it was only slightly higher ground.

At that point the wind was shifting to the east. The walls of the hurricane house were now shaking and the children were put to work to buttress the shelter. The water from the river was rising quickly and could be seen trespassing on the turnip fields and moving westward toward the northerly end of Cockeast Pond where another river was created about a quarter mile north of the herring run. If one was traveling from south to north along River Road on that day and could forge the herring run, one then would be halted by the flow of water between Cockeast Pond and the river.

While the children supported the walls with their weight, they could see large unmanned fishing boats from Tripp's Boat Yard and the wharf area at the Point being propelled toward their land. Boat after boat joined floats, sheds, and boathouses to the south in the harbor that washed up onto the Wheeler land. Then there was a knock at the Hurricane House door.

During the eye of the storm local college-aged friends had come from their homes in the Acoaxet area to help neighbors. They carried the children from the home as the wind and water were forces to be reckoned with and the entire clan finally found safety at the family year-round home where the summer tenants warmly welcomed them.

CHAPTER 12

Boathouse Row

There was more drama unfolding on Towne Avenue, now known as Boathouse Row. Boathouse Row is a west-to-east dirt road off Acoaxet Road in Westport Harbor along the channel at the entrance to the harbor. On the north side of the pot-holed, tenth-of-a-mile stretch along the river were about a dozen structures that were called boathouses, built on pilings and perched over the water. On the south side of the dirt road was the Charlton estate with its massive water tower, which was frequently climbed by local kids at night to enjoy the view. Some of the boathouses were large enough to have bedrooms but the owners and guests occupied them mostly during the day and they then served as teenage gathering spots at night. They functioned as launching sites for sailing, fishing and riverfront swimming from their wooden docks. The river between the Horseneck Point and Westport Harbor was jammed daily with fishing trawlers heading out to sea or back to the docks at the the Point with their catch as well as small and large pleasure craft like Ted Hebden's *Last Fling*, sailing vessels like the Brayton's schooner *Jane*, as well as water skiing enthusiasts. Near the most easterly point on the road there was a small area for river swimming for members of Elephant Rock Beach Club. There was also a small dock for members who did not own boathouses to come and tie up their dingy and row to their boats on moorings in the river. Next to that beach was the Barker boathouse, which was fairly sizeable, compared to other neighboring units. It was next to the rock outcropping, which was to the northwest of the Charlton Wharf. It was also across the road from the northeast section of the Charlton estate that was predominately reserved for the gardener's family house, potting shed and greenhouse. The gardener at the time was Herbert Branch who was the father of Janet, Paul, and Wayne, and he had a staff of three assistants. His wife, Edna Branch, was a teacher in the Westport School Department.

Herb asked his children to help take all the home's valuables to the second floor, as there was a hurricane on its way. The house was set back on a lot just west of the larger riverfront beach to the south of the wharf. The house was protected by a two-foot-high stonewall that surrounded the property. Wayne was also dispatched across the road to assist Harriet Barker, who had arrived early that morning to move clothes and anything of value to the second floor loft of their boathouse. With each passing moment the water was rising and Harriet needed to leave quickly to pass safely over Boathouse Row Road to Acoaxet Road to reach the safety of the Bliss home on Hurricane Lane.

When Wayne returned home from assisting Mrs. Barker, the water was gushing around the house and Herb issued an edict: "Get out in a hurry and take Taffy (a cocker spaniel puppy) with you," recalled Wayne.

As they exited the rear door to move to higher and safer ground at the brick and stone potting shed, Wayne said that the water was up to his knees and the hips of his mother, Edna. He looked to the southeast toward the Point of Rocks to see a massive wall of black water breaking over the far rocks and heading towards the family home. It was the same wall of black water that Eileen Sheehan was watching from farther up river. Today, Wayne calls it "a frightening image even for a cocky 14-year-old boy who was fearless of the water." From inside the potting shed the family could see nothing going on outside because the sheets of rain and wind had pasted leaves and twigs onto the windows preventing any visibility. As the eye passed, Wayne Branch looked to the north up the fast moving water of the west branch of the river. He noticed the absence of their families' twelve-by-eight play/bathhouse. It was gone along with camping gear and other valuables. As he looked up the river, he could see a couple of boathouses traveling north upside down on their roofs. One belonged to the Colby family.

Two days before the storm's arrival, 17-year-old Dick Colby drove his parents, George and Annabel, to Wickford, Rhode Island, to make boat connections to be transported to Galilee, Rhode Island. It was the first day of the annual Atlantic Tuna Club fishing tournament and over 100 deep-sea fishing vessels from up and down the east coast were trying to catch "the big one" in Rhode Island Sound. For many it was their last fling.

On Monday, August 30th the boats went out into a rough sea. On Tuesday half of the 140 boats sank at the dock or were driven inland as a result of Carol.

The senior Colby and his wife, Annabel, were not able to return to their family for two more days, but George Colby did manage to catch a ride on a seaplane that landed in the Westport River.

Young Colby was at home at the family house with his two sisters, Susan and Marcia. Their home on Atlantic Avenue sat diagonally across the road from Elephant Rock Beach Club and within view of the Cozy Cab bus as it revved its motor prior to taking its final trip across the macadam strip. Upon waking and seeing the outside conditions, Dick jumped into a family car and drove less than a quarter-mile to the family boathouse which was co-owned with the Potter Cunningham family. The boathouse had only been purchased a year earlier in 1953 from the Maker family for a mere $5,000. It

Westport River boathouse destroyed.
(Photo courtesy of The Herald News)

was only down the road and he went to remove items of value. As he left the structure at 9 a.m. the rising river was lapping just underneath the first floor boards. Fifteen minutes later his friend, Wayne Branch, watched the small house flip off its wooden pilings onto its roof and float north up the river. It was completely destroyed, but the family eventually retrieved their floating dock, which had completed its journey up river to make a landing on shore on the Wheeler property next to Ben's Point.

A few days later Dick and his Dad and a man named Orel MacDuff reached the property to retrieve their boathouse remains. They not only found the floating dock but flooring from the Elephant Rock Pavilion which had washed up the length of Cockeast Pond on the west side of River Road and then was carried by the receding river water across the road onto the Wheeler property adjacent to the river. They used a number of the flooring planks "to skid the dock back into the river and then with a temporary bracket installed on the dock, we mounted a 1-1/2 horsepower outboard motor which enabled me to drive it down river back to where it was moored," reported Dick Colby.

They never found the remnants of the boathouse. They built a new structure.

Eight–year-old Charlotte Brayton Underwood watched the storm with her mother, Katie, who did not feel comfortable around the water at all since she grew up inland in Pennsylvania. They were joined by Charlotte's younger siblings, Anne and Roswell, and their cousin, Lee Katzenbach, as the river exploded under their feet in their boathouse sanctuary. The family watched neighbors remove their boats from floats and moorings to the Charlton fields to the south. They served as a communication link to many, as their boathouse was the only one on the river with a telephone. The group watched Harriet Barker drive up the road to safety.

It was their father's sister, Aunt Charlotte Brayton, whose house overlooked the Elephant Rock Beach Club parking lot who arrived to direct them to higher ground at her brother, Uncle Philip's house at the northernmost part of Cockeast Pond. Charlotte thinks that they were in the last car over the herring run before the road collapsed, rendering the Acoaxet portion of Westport Harbor an island. From Philip's house high on a rock, they could look back down into the river and see the boats breaking from their moorings and grounding themselves in the river flats and on the shoreline. They watched the porches and entire structures, contents and all, break up and float away to be claimed by others up river. Some structures floated up river on their roofs including the "Shearpin" which was owned by George Ashworth and Madison Welch. Next door was George Colby's boathouse.

When the storm was over the Brayton clan stayed where they were for a few days until power was restored but Katie and her kids did not return to the boathouse and a year later her husband, Roswell, constructed a home for the family further north on River Road but removed from the dangers of flooding.

Another Brayton family member, Flint, was less timid. On the day of the storm, which he had followed with newspaper and radio reports over the prior couple of days, he awoke his wife, Hope and their three children, Suze, 12, Paul, 9, and Carol, 7 and rushed them from the safety of their home three miles north to watch the surf. Flint ushered his family into the car before 8 a.m. and drove to Boathouse Row and parked in front of his family boathouse where his sister, Edith, was staying. She was located adjacent to Roz and Katie

Water rises on Boathouse Row.
(Photo courtesy of Suze Brayton)

Brayton's place. Flint wanted to see the surf breaking in the mouth of the harbor next to the Point of Rocks. With the wind biting and the rain and sand nipping at their skin, they quickly turned around and returned to his sister, Edith, in the boathouse.

The volume of water in the river had risen dramatically. The windows in the boathouse began to implode. Katie and her sister–in–law, Charlotte, were leaving and Harriet Barker had already departed. The Branch family had headed for safer, higher ground. Flint packed his family back into the car and persuaded Edith to retreat with them to his house closer to Adamsville. Off they all went west on Boathouse Row to River Road to escape the rising waters that soon collapsed the asphalt over the herring run creating the Acoaxet Island. They were one of the final Brayton cars over the gushing water.

Westport, Massachusetts

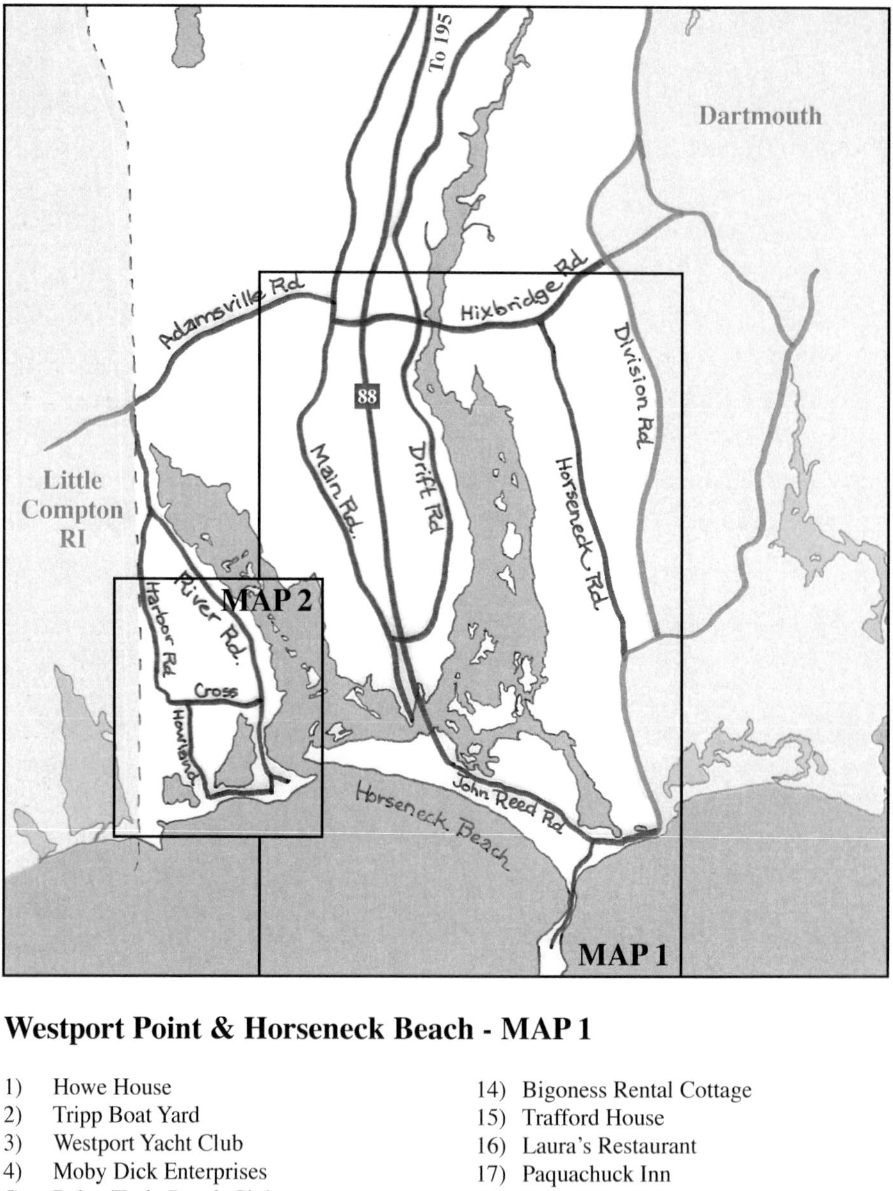

Westport Point & Horseneck Beach - MAP 1

1) Howe House
2) Tripp Boat Yard
3) Westport Yacht Club
4) Moby Dick Enterprises
5) Baker/Earle Beach Club
6) Spindrift/Plante's Pavilion
7) Gendreau's Concession Stand
8) Souza House
9) Hazen House
10) Sisson House
11) Quonset Huts/Portuguesse Village
12) Observation Tower
13) Nick "The Greek's" Bar
14) Bigoness Rental Cottage
15) Trafford House
16) Laura's Restaurant
17) Paquachuck Inn
18) Stone Wharf
19) Town Wharf
20) Lees Wharf and Store
21) DeNadal House
22) Noquachoke Orchards
23) St John's Catholic Church
24) Westport Town Hall
25) Lees Market
26) BayCoast Bank

Westport Point & Horseneck Beach - MAP 1 & 1A

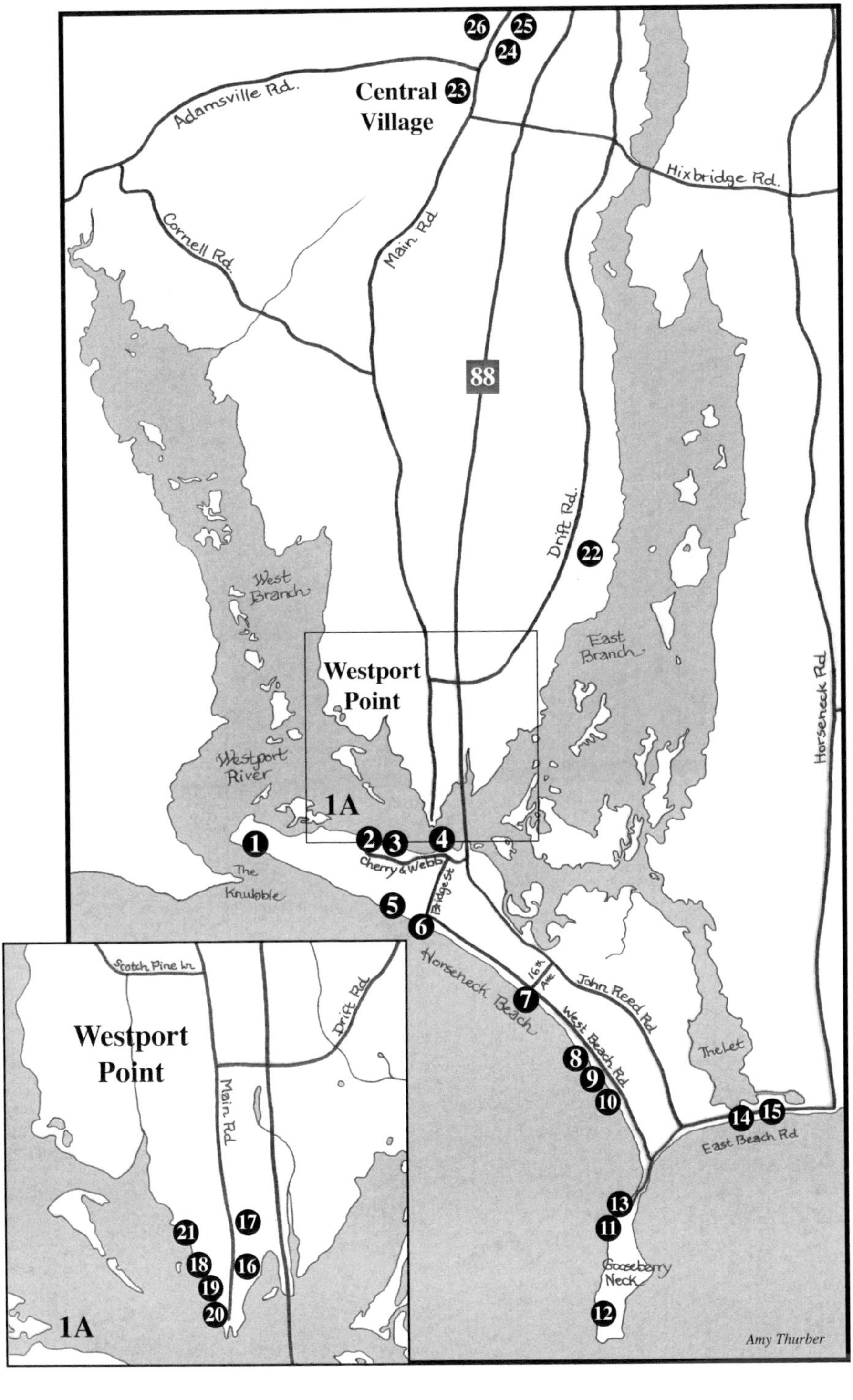

CHAPTER 13

The Bridge

"And I, cut off from the world, remain
Alone with the terrible hurricane."

"Hurricane"
W.C. Bryant

According to reports more than 3,000 boats were smashed, beached or sunk in Massachusetts as a result of Carol's fury. One half of the boats in the New Bedford/Fairhaven fishing fleet were damaged. In Westport many of the nautical victims ended smashed up at the Westport Point Bridge and the dock area including Ted Hebden's sport fishing vessel, *The Last Fling*, which only the day before had been our family's fishing boat.

It was flung stem to stern onto the dock. Across the channel at the Westport Yacht Club and at Tripp's Boat Yard vessels of all types and sizes had broken free from moorings and docks and were strewn about the landscape. Many were moved by the current but against the east wind and headed up river toward the bridge and its abutments.

"Jack Brayton and I watched the Brayton family's beautiful, black sailboat, the *Jane*, break its mooring, float down the river, hit the old bridge, and sink. We watched all this from my parent's second floor bedroom," recounted Sheila DeNadal Salvo, sixteen at the time and herself a Westport survivor of GH38.

The Last Fling on Town Wharf.
(Photo courtesy of The Herald News*)*

In 1954, the DeNadal family home was near the docks on the west side of the lowest end of Main Road and was used as hurricane central by Westport and State Police alike.

Albert E Lees Sr. bought the wharf and fish market in 1930, he served as the bridge's draw master and was paid $150 per year for the next 30 years. His son, Al Lees, Jr. took over the position for two more years until a new bridge was built along with a new access highway to the east of the wharf to the state - controlled Horseneck Beach in 1958. Main Road then became a dead-end and businesses like Lees Fish Market and the nearby Paquachuck Inn were no longer located on a busy thoroughfare. Lees moved his market up Main Road and eventually constructed a modern grocery market in Central Village where it operates today under the direction of his son, Albert E. Lees III.

The old wooden bridge span provided passage to the Horseneck side of the river and to the east passage of the river. It was finally demolished in 1962 amid as much angst as when it was proposed. The original bridge was built in 1893 amid a great deal of controversy - townspeople voted to reject the idea on two occasions, but wealthy people from New Bedford and Fall River who owned summer cottages on Horseneck Beach prevailed upon the state to overrule local objections. In the late nineteenth century, a New Bedford engineer, Z.B. Davis, designed the structure.

The first bridge was 782 feet long. The 30 foot manually controlled swing span draw was opened with a large "key" and wooden pole. It took four men, Lees and three local volunteers who hung around the wharf, to operate the draw, which allowed those who made appointments in advance to have the link open at a specific time. As a reward, Lees provided the volunteers with complimentary soft drinks and snacks after the job was completed. On average there were only 15 openings per year over the deepest part of the channel near Lees Fish Market. It stretched from the wharf near Laura's Restaurant and the Paquachuck Inn over the river to an area just east and south of the Moby Dick Restaurant, now known as the Back Eddy, and the other local enterprises. Not only was it a travel convenience, it attracted throngs of fishermen to a spot many called the best salt water fishing in New England. Nightly, strangers gathered side by side to cast their lines into the rapidly flowing river channel's current in hopes of catching stripers when they were biting.

The town paid the cost of maintaining the bridge over the years but after "The Long Island Express" slammed into it in 1938, the state paid for the needed repairs. Every two years the town needed to replace the wooden planks on the bridge at a cost of $2,500 for materials alone. One year a laborer from the town public works department became so sea sick while working on the viaduct watching the rushing current below him that he needed to be reassigned to a land job by his boss, according to Fred Cambra who started working for the town at age 18 in 1951. (The life-long town resident ran the Highway Department from 1962-71 and retired in 1990.)

After World War II, vehicular traffic to the beach increased dramatically over the bridge and long lines of cars created traffic jams in the quaint fishing village. Residents like the DeNadals were unhappy because they could barely get out of their driveway to access the road, but businesses on the north side of the bridge such as Leach Marine, Lees Fish Market, Laura's Restaurant and The Paquachuck Inn were thriving.

Over the bridge to the south, Sheldon "Pappy" Judson was carving out his own seasonal enterprises, using the Moby Dick name. It was certainly appropriate as Westport followed nearby New Bedford, Massachusetts into the whaling business with as many as 30 whalers operating out of the Point in the mid to late 1800's, according to Carmen Maiocco in his 1992 booklet, Westport Point Bridge. Judson operated a sandwich shop, a Gulf gas station, a fish market, and

(Postcard courtesy of Albert E. Lees Jr. collection)

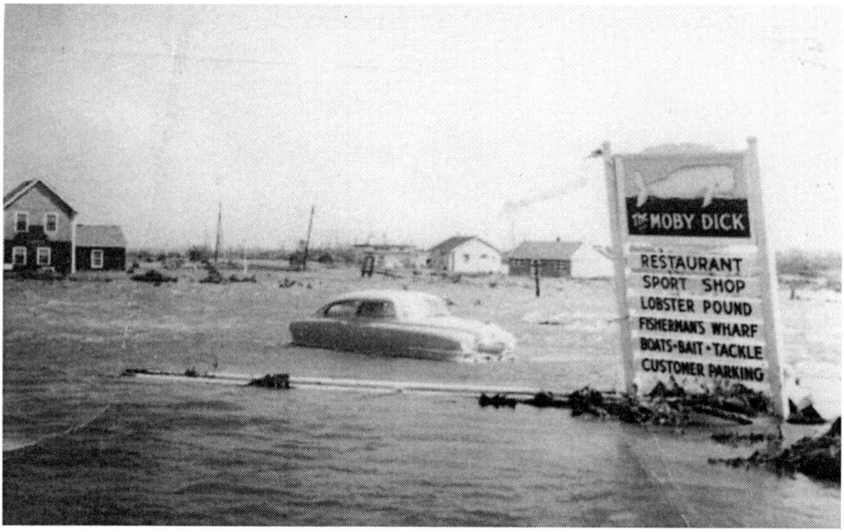

Moby Dick Enterprises under water.
(Photo courtesy of the New Bedford Standard Times)

a lobster pound along with customer parking and a sportswear shop owned by his daughter, Norma.

The bridge facilitated enterprises like Tripp's Boat Yard and Baker and Earle's Beach as well as the construction of the Westport Yacht Club and a number of homes built on West Beach Road on Horseneck Beach.

The bathhouses at Baker and Earle's Beach, now known as Baker's Beach for nearly 40 years, was destroyed and rebuilt three times. The bathhouses fell victim to the "Long Island Express" in 1938 and then again in 1944. After each hurricane, more units were added and built in clusters of 12. There were 16 units-192 individual bath houses turned upside down and scattered throughout the dunes after Carol came and went, according to Harbormaster Richie Earle whose father owned the bathing beach at the time. Richie recalls checking on the cabanas late in the day on August 31, 1954, and seeing waves breaking out in the ocean as far as you could see.

Carol ravages Baker and Earle Beach bathhouses.
(Photo courtesy of Sue and Lynn Carter)

"It howled and shrieked, almost all day'" he recalled.

Louis McHenry Howe maintained a summer place on Horseneck Beach. He acted as an advisor (in fact, he served as the President's Secretary which today equates to Chief–of -Staff) and close friend to President Franklin Delano Roosevelt. FDR was a visitor to Howe's home located in the dunes at the west end of the beach almost at Horseneck Point, which was the most extreme point on the west end of Horseneck Beach at the mouth of the harbor. It overlooked the Charlton estate on the other side of the mouth of the river and ocean. The President traveled by horse-drawn carriage over the sand at low tide from Plante's Pavilion, later known as the Spindrift located at the end of Bridge Road, to his advisor's summer retreat.

Families from as far away as Boston would drive to Horseneck Beach for the day during the heat of the summer. They needed to arrive early to get a parking spot at either Spindrift or Midway Restaurants.

Both had large parking lots, changing rooms, as well as rest rooms and concessions. Both enterprises employed lifeguards who patrolled their respective beachfronts. The Plante family lived on the second floor above the commercial eating establishment and would be in for quite a ride before the summer of '54 was to end. But before Hurricane Carol was ever a spot on the radar in the Caribbean or made a move north, the Commonwealth of Massachusetts had its eye on the prime oceanfront coastline. Plans were being developed to take over the beach and put it under state control, build a new access highway - Route 88 - from the Fall River line in north Westport southerly to the ocean. It was a straight shot except a new bridge needed to be constructed to the east of the original span in order to better accommodate the expected influx of visitors.

Hurricane Carol gave the state just what it needed: a public reason to fulfill its private plan. Carol destroyed vessels of all sizes, some of which slammed into the bridge. Wind and water took out the Judson enterprises as well as Laura's Restaurant and caused major harm to the Yacht Club and Tripp's Boat Yard as well as the hundreds of homes on Horseneck, East and West Beach and Gooseberry Neck.

Late on the same afternoon after Carol struck, the Souza family joined others who had evacuated and walked back over the viaduct and along the same path they had departed earlier that day. But Fred Cambra from the Highway Department was already there in the roadway along with the sand and rocks and contents of homes and white foam from the ocean. It was a mess.

Operating a bulldozer all night and into the next day, Fred had cleared a path on the road which permitted homeowners to return temporarily to collect personal effects.

Clearing sand from Horseneck roadways.
(Photo courtesy of Westport Historical Society)

Fred, who was only 21 and the father of three at the time, had been working non-stop more than 24 hours. Initially sent out at three o'-clock in the morning to the north end of town to clear broken tree limbs from wires and roadways, he and his other crewmembers progressed in a southerly direction during the day. Late in the day after the water receded at the end of Main Road they were given the go-ahead from the National Guard stationed at the entrance to the bridge to move heavy equipment very cautiously over the bridge. Holes in the road on the south side of the bridge made from rising high water needed to be filled prior to transporting the heavy equipment to the beach. After driving his bulldozer over the bridge, Fred needed to maneuver the obstacle course through debris and even around homes in the John Reed and West Beach roadways. The storm surge caused the most damage, bringing tons of sand from the dunes into the roads. Fred set out to clear a path for police and fire emergency vehicles.

Unlike many of their neighbors, Doctor Souza and his family found their house still upright. Utility wires, still attached to adjacent poles, were in the middle of West Beach Road, helping to hold it up. Although it had been spun around like a top, the inside stayed in place - the milk bottle without a drop missing - was still sitting on the table from breakfast. Board games remained on the shelves but Lois' two painted turtles, Gloria and Pinky, were no longer resting in their plastic dish on the kitchen floor. They were free! They had been replaced with debris from the storm.

Fred kept plowing sand back into the dunes. He would work for many nights under the light of a full moon.

"There was nothing but sand on West Beach Road from the Spindrift all the way to Sixteenth Avenue where the Midway Snack Bar used to be. It was wiped out. The sand was so piercing it was blasting the paint off the bulldozer. From there over to Gooseberry there were homes and sheds all over the road," he recalled.

After passing the Souza house, which had been spun around from west-to-north-facing, Fred encountered another challenge: a house suspended by utility wires over the road. This presented a unique but solvable problem for the young but veteran town employee. The exhaust pipe from his town dozer rose in a vertical direction from the engine, not horizontally, as a tail pipe from the rear. He could not pass under the house without hitting the exhaust pipe. But with tools for any job, Fred removed, then reattached, the pipe and was able to keep moving forward. It took nearly three straight days of moving sand to open passage for house-moving firms to be able to access structures in order to reposition them off the road back to the area from whence they had come.

There was treasure to be had for the hard-working young men of the town highway department. They plowed the roads day after day, spending months clearing and re-clearing as the sand and the wind shifted direction. Periodically, the Red Cross would arrive with their canteen to provide coffee and donuts for the workers. The workers also uncovered items of interest, like six-packs of beer. The crew would rebury their treasures in the sand for future consumption, for as Cambra called it, "medicinal purposes." For weeks as Cambra and his town co-workers continued to move the sand off the roads, it seemed to be everywhere. Cambra would pack his lunch, put it into a metal lunch box and then put the box inside a paper bag, but the sand still found its way into his sandwich.

CHAPTER 14

The Other Jimmy

While Jimmy Graham and his bus passengers were losing the fight with the ocean surge on Atlantic Avenue in the Harbor, there was lots of action at the Point. The water from the storm swell in the river was lifting boats, buildings and even planes off their moorings and foundations. The wind and water - some estimated the current in the river was running at 20 knots - displaced boats and even destroyed a seaplane owned by "Cukie" Macomber, a fellow named William Healey and two others who would fly tourists on trips to the islands. Twenty-nine–year-old Macomber who had survived "The Long Island Express" rose at 5:30 that morning and drove his car to the river along with the other plane owners when they heard a storm was approaching. The winds had reached 55 miles per hour. They needed to fill the plane's floats with water so it would not blow away. At 60 miles per hour the plane would lift by itself even without a pilot on board. It did not. Eventually, it just sank!

His sword fishing boat that he operated and owned with his father looked secure on the mooring so the group headed home only to be isolated on Cherry and Webb Lane by the rising water level. His car went underwater and Macomber and his pals were now stuck in the sand dunes on Horseneck Beach with winds coming out of the east at 100 plus miles per hour and blowing sand cutting into their faces. They noticed a wharf float from either Tripp's Boat Yard or the Westport Yacht Club moving up the river and saw it cut the mooring line to their swordfish boat. They watched helplessly as the current took the boat up river into the granite pier of the drawbridge and smashed into pieces.

On that day Macomber lost just about everything, "my car was underwater, my seaplane was wrecked and my swordfish boat was gone. I sat down and bawled my head off", he said in the Westport Shorelines when interviewed on the 50th anniversary of the hurricane in 2004. At that event, "Cukie" said, "We will never have a hurricane like that again." He meant that we would never be surprised by a hurricane like that again.

At nearby Tripp's Boat Yard owner Bill Tripp had no idea a storm was nearing until the river water was four to six feet high in his parking lot. The water rose over his docks and boat lines slipped off the pilings, sending craft off on their own into the rushing water. Some boats ended up in the marsh while others found their way into the bridge abutments or docks up river. The boatyard crew watched as one of their main sheds with all its contents just disintegrated. Tripp and many of his boat yard staff joined Macomber and others in the dunes despite the fact that dunes were sandwiched between the ocean and river. Tripp recalled that as many as 40 people survived the '38 hurricane by heading into the dunes. This time a number of pigs that resided on Cherry and Webb Lane joined the humans seeking refuge in the dunes. When they returned to the boatyard, they recorded the high water mark on the same shed where GH38 was recorded but at approximately one foot HIGHER.

Residents of the Point had moved down Main Road toward the bridge and the three docks - Lees, the town, and what was known as the "stone heap" - to witness Mother Nature's fury. The George Smith family trudged across the bridge at 10 a.m. as the last family to make it from the Horseneck side. By then, water was up to their knees, as they sloshed past Laura's Restaurant and the Paquachuck Inn heading north for higher ground past disbelieving onlookers near the DeNadal home on Main Road.

It was shortly after then that Laura's Restaurant broke away and began to float up river. Two employees, Natalie Silva, age 20, a waitress, and 64–year-old, Harry Macomber, a kitchen helper, were spotted in the lower level of the building screaming for help. That sight sent others into the water for a rescue. The employees, upon reaching the safety of shore, screamed, "The bartender is still out there."

Sixty-four–year-old Jim Hickey was spotted hanging out of the second floor window of the bar section of the building. But no one was making a move to save Hickey. It was simple. The men did not like the crotchety, old bartender and he held the bar tab records. None of the local men wanted Hickey or the records back. More innocent youngsters, like 15-year-old Paul DeNadal, Sheila's brother, and William White, jumped into a skiff to go save Jim. By the time they reached him on the south side of the building, salt spray and foam covered their faces and the water was up to Jim's chin. He was barely able to keep his head above water while rats were jumping out the windows all around him. Even during the rescue, Hickey was trying to save a strong box presumably with the bar's I.O.U.'s. Hickey was saved, sent to the hospital, but the bar tabs were never recovered despite the fact, that the building ended up on a mudflat and never did sink completely. The building sat there for a couple of years before one hot summer evening there was a tragic, unexpected bonfire out in the river and Laura's Restaurant finally was no more. The fire department had been alerted in advance not to rush to put out the fire.

"Curiosity killed the cat..." as the saying goes but fortunately, none of the Westporters who ventured out to the causeway at Gooseberry Neck suffered the same fate on August 31, 1954.

Laura's employees rescued.
(Photo courtesy of Paul and Cecile DeNadal)

Gooseberry was originally an island until a causeway connecting it to Horseneck was built in 1924. From the mid-point on Horesneck Beach to the farthest point of Gooseberry Neck out in the ocean, it is a distance of nearly two miles but the promontory is only a few hundred yards wide at its widest point. The one-lane roadway and the island suffered significant damage in GH38 and then again in 1944.

In 1944, the peninsular served as a military coastal defense installation. The land had been taken over and the causeway enlarged by the government after the bombing of Pearl Harbor in 1941. The government built a surveillance tower that resembled a silo along with a farmhouse and barn to house troops on the Neck. There was a guardhouse at the entrance to the causeway at the intersection of East and West Beach Roads. Well into the late 1940's, owners of houses on Horseneck were instructed by the military to turn off all lights at night and the beach was patrolled both on land and from the ocean to enforce the rules. Soldiers knocked at the door of the Souza house one evening as a sliver of light could be seen by a patrol boat through a bathroom blackout shade. Young Charlie had been reading in the bathroom. He was ordered to extinguish the light. That put an end to his reading for that night.

By 1954 the troops had departed from Gooseberry Neck but summer shacks and large sleeping M.A.S.H.- like tents joined Quonset huts and summer folk, like the Benjamin family. They couldn't find a more idyllic place to stay - until August 31, 1954. According to Leo "Checkered Moon" Benjamin, as the wind, rain and surf picked up many Neck residents headed for the safety of the cement observation tower. The tower had provided National Guard troops a wonderful vantage point to observe any German submarine spy activity during and after World War II. It also allowed Neck residents a safe haven during the hurricane. Three residents of the Neck were found safe in the tower the day following the storm.

Towns-people called that area "Portuguese Village" since many a shack was constructed for storage of fishing gear. The Portuguese community in the area was beginning to thrive because so many came from a heritage of farming and fishing and found Westport an ideal place to settle. Those on the island could be considered "squatters" since the government owned the land and never sold off any of it.

The curious from farther inland headed to the causeway to watch Mother Nature's anger on display in full force. Walter Vincent, Bill Hart and Roger Reed were just three who ventured to the causeway and had stories to tell.

Vincent arrived at 8 a.m. before things really started to pop. It was early morning and prior to the opening of Nick "The Greek's" bar. Nick and his brother Charlie ran the establishment on the Neck at the end of the causeway. Despite, it being public property, the brothers would charge 25 cents per auto to cross. As the cars approached, Charlie would leave his post at the bar and run out to collect the quarter, which everyone seemed willing to pay. The Westport kids had that figured out. A carload of young people would arrive, pay Charlie and go in for a beverage while the driver would return to pick up more friends. When the car returned, Charlie again left his station and went out to get his quarter. That move left the bar unattended and gave the kids the opportunity to help themselves to the stock at hand.

By 8:30 that morning the Quonset hut where Vincent and some others were hanging out began to shake. Vincent realized the military housing was not going to make it.

And it didn't.

He had a carful of friends that morning, as he often did at night when they hung out at Nick's Bar, and he carefully backed up over the causeway. With headwinds and water rising, it made a successful return dubious. Walter needed to be creative to survive. He instructed his passengers to roll down the windows thereby changing the pressure inside the vehicle and duck down in the car to lower the resistance, which was enough to propel them back to the mainland, allowing a safe return.

Hart and Reed had similar haunting stories. Both went to the causeway to see the action. And both came close to not making it back after a quick observation that clearly they should not be there. With waves breaking over the causeway and surf spray towering over utility poles, both young men separately came to the same conclusion: "We better get out of here."

As Hart tried to back up his car, it stalled and he panicked. The engine was not turning over as waves slapped against its side. Having spent years on the water, Hart knew when to abandon ship or in this case, car. It was time.

"This was no place to be. I ran like a ----," he said in a Shorelines newspaper interview on the occasion of the 50th anniversary held at the Paquachuck Inn. His car was found after the storm with his skiff's outboard motor in the trunk, the entire vehicle crushed by rocks. But its occupants were safe!

Reed and his teenager pals needed some ingenuity to survive as well. His 1937 Ford would not start either after they had reached the causeway parking lot. After pushing it up the road with doors open

Lives being saved at Westport Point
(Photo courtesy of The Herald News*)*

to benefit from the strong winds, they reached a spot that lost the wind. Thankfully, a milkman was still delivering on his early morning rounds and Reed and his pals convinced the driver to give them a push far enough down the road enabling the car to get a jump-start and proceed to his second adventure of the morning: helping to save the lives of those floating up river in Laura's Restaurant.

Augustus Robbilard joined Reed and Paul Denadal in a rowboat and they saved the waitress and the cook from certain death. The teens and their rowboat were pulled back to the Point by other townspeople on shore. Then it was just a day's work for the kids, until they looked back upon it.

CHAPTER 15

The Real Tragedy-Victims

Hurricane Carol in Westport resulted in major devastation but fortunately there was minimum loss of life. Two-year-old baby, Mark Bigoness of Hartford, Connecticut, drowned off East Beach. Leo Beaulieu, who was working at the main entrance of the Lincoln Park dance hall in the northeast section of town on the Westport / Dartmouth town line far from the ravages of the water on the day after the storm, died when a tree limb he was cutting fell and killed him. More than 100 local people were injured and a list of names of residents with their addresses who were treated at the four local hospitals in Fall River - Union, Truesdale, St. Anne's and General - was placed on the front page of the The Herald News - for all to read.

On that day in Westport, seventy-four–year-old James Ferguson died of natural causes, and two–year-old Mark Bigoness, the hurricane victim, was one of only two deaths associated with the storm. No one was married and there were no births recorded. There were too many other things going on!

The Bigoness story is the real tragedy of the hurricane. Unlike GH38 when 22 died in Westport, Carol only claimed two lives. While it was sad that Leo Beaulieu died as a result of injuries suffered while clearing debris the day after the storm, the death of an older person does not evoke the same emotion as the tragic loss of a child.

Mark Bigoness came to Westport with his parents, Fred, age 35 and his wife, Paola, age 33 and Mark's brother, Stephen, age 4. Friends, Felix and Edna Lazarin and their two sons, Edward and Steven, joined them. It was to be an end-of-the-summer vacation in an East Beach four-bedroom, oceanfront cottage for the two hard-working

Connecticut families. Fred was a machinist who also made stained glass windows for Hartford area churches and he was looking forward all year to taking his young family to the ocean for a week's holiday. A family friend from Connecticut had offered them the use of his oceanfront cottage in Westport.

Like so many others, Bigoness and his family and friends had no advance warning of the storm and, living inland as they did, they were not familiar with the power of the wind and water.

On the morning of the storm, Stephen Bigoness recalls, "My father yelled, 'We have to get out' because the cottage was starting to break in half and float away." They attempted to reach their car but it was partially underwater by the time they evacuated. The party of eight went wading through the water to reach a safe area. The next thing he recalls is being lifted into a tree by his dad and being told not to move. Fred then left his son and went to assist his wife who was holding baby Mark. After exiting the house, Paola became entrapped in wire and was unable to hold her baby over her head any longer. A massive wave came and swept the baby out of his mother's grasp and away from his parents only to be found hours later at night by bulldozer operator, Fred Cambra, as he cleared the roads of sand and debris.

There was sadness in his clearing work. "It was eerie," he said, "We did not know what we were going to find." The crew unearthed a body in the road that first night of the two–year-old baby. The baby was one of only two people in Westport whose deaths were attributed to the hurricane.

Others living on high ground took in the Bigoness and Lazarin families until the frantic parents could go back out to look for their child. Sadly, it was too late. And so the parents' worst nightmare - the loss of their child - became a reality that has lasted a lifetime. The Bigoness family who still live in Connecticut never returned to Westport.

Westport Harbor and Acoaxet-
MAP 2 & 2A

1) Acoaxet Club
2) Howland House & Farm
3) Smith House
4) Water Tower
5) Cummings House
6) Hindley House
7) Hanson House
8) Eastwood House
9) Rodgers House
10) Sturdevannt Dog House
11) Foster Bath Houses
12) Howland Bath Houses
13) Eastwood Beach House
14) Shaw House
15) Richardson House
16) Eddy House
17) Knowles House
18) D'Angelo House
19) Rhee House
20) Potter and Otte Houses
21) Gallery House
22) Cockeast Pond, Gull Rock
23) Dr. French's Steps
24) Elephant Rock Beach Club
25) Snow House
26) Colby House
27) McDuff House
28) Pond Meadow-Charlton Estate
29) Round House-The Keep
30) Branch House
31) Barker Boat House
32) Brayton Boat Houses
33) Ogden Store/Harbor Inn
34) Casino
35) Herring Run
36) Spindle Rock Restuarant
37) Sheehan Houses
38) Tripp/Bojuma Farm
39) Coggeshall House
40) Acoaxet Chapel
41) Pelton House
42) Bryan House
43) Phinney House
44) Borden House

MAP 2

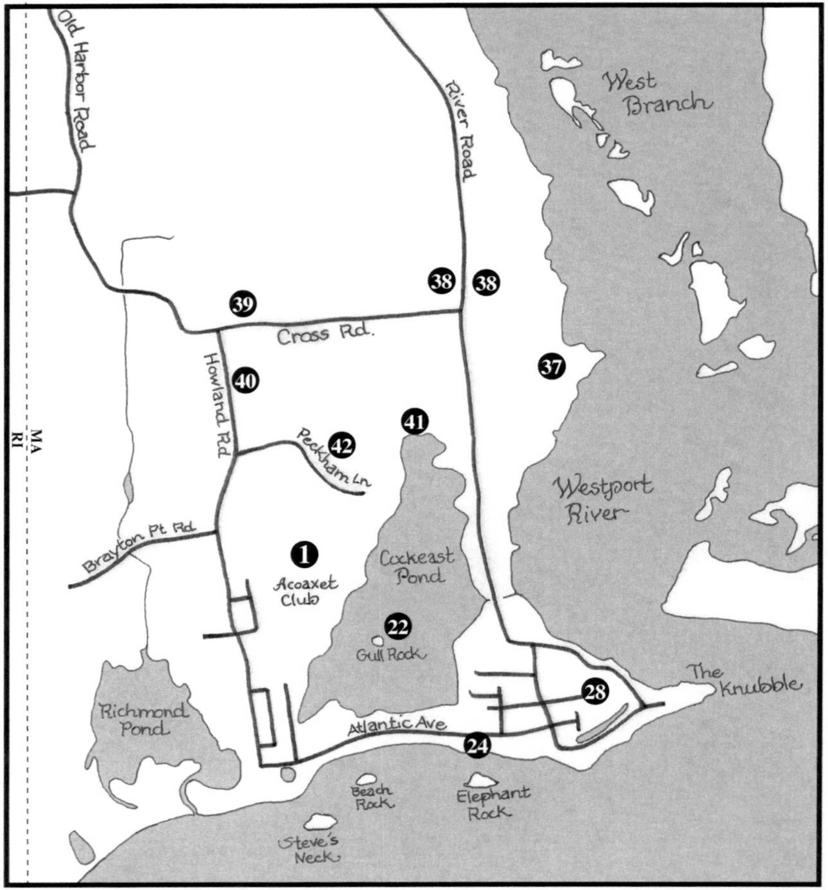

Westport Harbor and Acoaxet - MAP 2 A

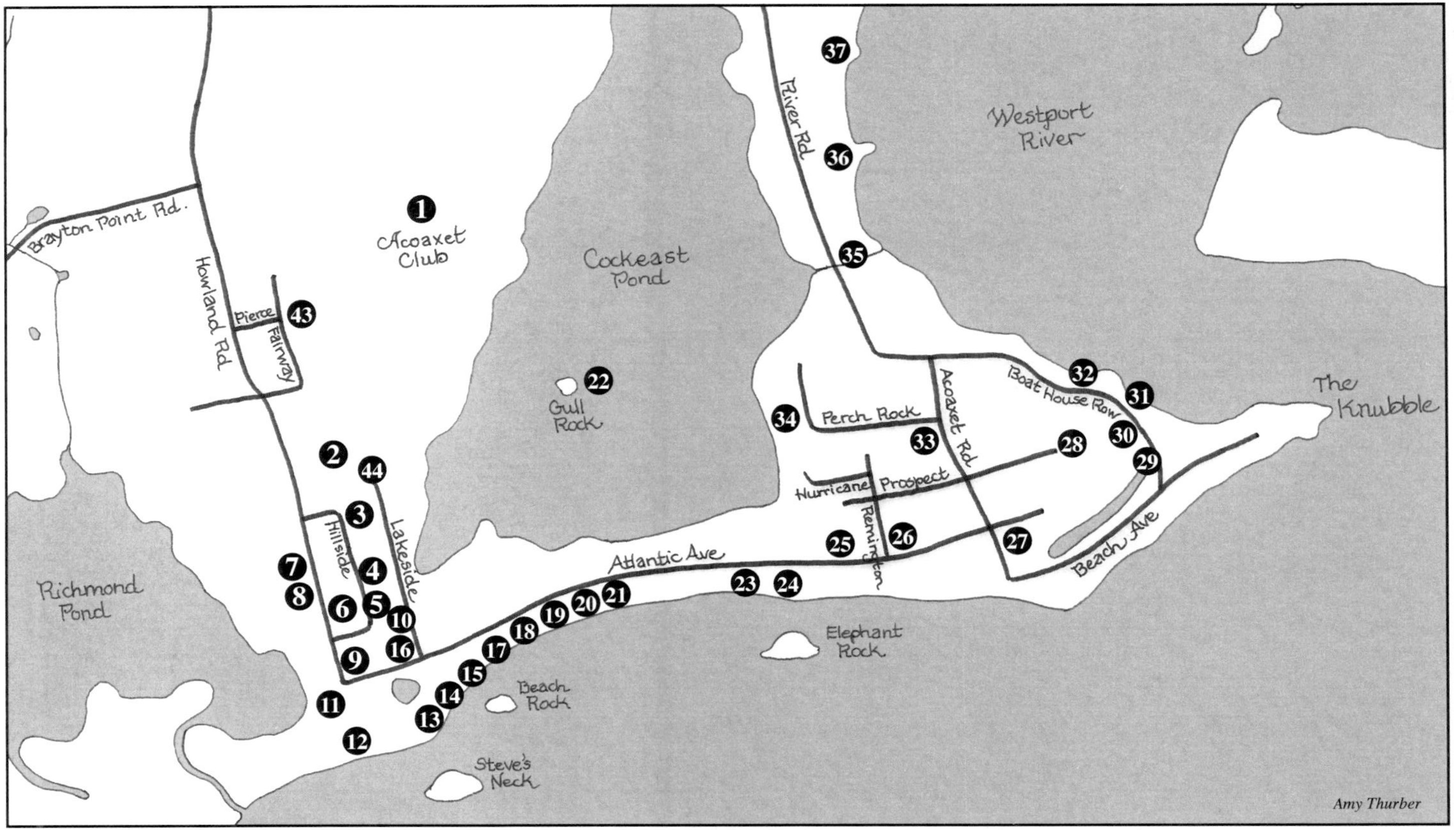

– Part Three –

CHAPTER 16

The Aftermath

When the cyclone subsided enough to venture out of the Acoaxet clubhouse in mid-afternoon, we found that the tide had risen 10 feet above normal and more than 2.31 inches of rain had fallen. The wind had continued from the south and southeast three hours past the eye, an unusually long time. It swung into the southwest and continued from that direction from 2 p.m. until dark and then changed to northwest.

By late in the day, the bus remained in Cockeast Pond with just its roof and upper portion of windows visible. The pond was like the nets of a fishing trawler catching and holding in its grasp anything

The Janice B on the town dock at the point.
(Photo courtesy of The Herald News*)*

that entered its confines. It not only caught a bus but homes and bathhouses, refrigerators and automobiles and jewelry.

Most of us went back to our homes to survey the damage but were soon joined by others - sightseers who were beginning to descend like locusts. It was necessary for the local police, followed by the National Guard, to secure the area and protect it from looters. Only those who could prove they were residents were permitted into disaster areas to inspect and secure their possessions.

My parents and I left the Acoaxet clubhouse and walked along the entrance drive that was covered with chestnut tree leaves like a massive brown carpet. The three-story edifice was east of the two tennis courts and the tennis practice backboard on the premises. The wood-framed back screens behind each end of the courts were folded up

The Gallery home foundation on the beach in the foreground and the house-within the circle left- in the pond abutting the golf course fairway. The Vanderburgh house stands intact. (Photo courtesy of Lorna Phan and Holly Bronhard from the Dr. Tony D'Angelo collection)

like an accordion and limbs from the once-mighty chestnut trees were strewn all over what was then the third hole on the golf course. The hole ran east to west toward Howland Road from the clubhouse. From the clubhouse we could see houses in the pond on the banks of the sixth and eighth fairways that only hours before were secure on the beach.

The Gallery house was there, a two-story structure, which had been on the beach across from the Vanderburgh house on Atlantic Avenue. Mrs. Katherine Vanderburgh and her daughter had purchased their home in 1951 and it was the only house on the north side bordering Cockeast Pond between the Elephant Rock Beach Club parking lot and Lakeside Avenue. The rose colored concrete slab of the Gallery house split by the power of the water is still visible in the sand over a half-century later. Three other beachfront homes belonging to Shaw, Otte and Potter (their flower vase was still upright on the dining table) rested near the Gallery house in the brackish pond water.

Prior to Labor Day weekend activities, Phinney allowed employee Sonny Carter and his uncle to remove the Gallery's matchstick like structure for scrap. It was reassembled months later on the Carter land as a garage, according to Sonny, now age 86 and still riding his bike on the country roads.

When we reached Howland Road and headed south, we found ourselves forging over tree limbs, downed wires and uprooted, snapped-in-half hundred-year-old trees. We reached the Howland House at the top of the hill and in the distance saw the beach for the first time since the storm hit. It looked like a war zone. Leaves were stripped from the trees and the swans had left the ponds to travel inland for protection. (But there was little safety inland as trees that slanted in one direction when the storm arrived were flipped in the opposite direction like toggle switches when the wind shifted. And then they uprooted.)

Most of Hillside Road was devoid of homes. The Steve Howland cow barn was on the north corner of Hillside and Howland Roads. There were no structures from the northerly entrance of Hillside Road all the way around the west side of the road until the southerly access was reached.

Steve Howland had used all the vacant land at one time as a garden to grow and sell his vegetables to the locals. Howland laid out his building subdivision with 9,800-square-foot lots in 1950, but most were not developed until after Carol. In fact, the lots along the west side of Hillside Road commencing at the corner of Hillside and Howland across from the cow barn were sold to people like Sturges Richardson whose prefab house on the beach crossed Atlantic Avenue before it was eventually moved to the top of Hillside Road.

Howland Hazen, Bill Priestly, Eleanor Roberts and Doctor Charles Souza, whose homes had been partially destroyed by Carol in the Horseneck and West Beach areas, were transported by flatbed truck over winding narrow roads over 15 miles to a parcel of land owned by Steve Howland and put on cinder-block foundations on Hillside Road. The Souza "hurricane proof" house came complete with the original refrigerator and bathtub and bathroom window. The window and tub are still in place in 2011. It turned out that the contractor who made the outlandish claim was fairly close to being on target as the main part of the structure did survive and was transported to its new location. The Hazen house came to its new site complete with hurricane sand that had infiltrated the space between the roof and ceiling but was not discovered until years later when a contractor removed the ceiling to make repairs and was showered in Horseneck Beach/Hurricane Carol sand.

That group of former Horseneck/West Beach residents along with the Cooper family moved to Westport Harbor only because in the fall of 1955 after the summer season ended the Commonwealth of

Massachusetts, under the leadership of Governor Christian Herter, informed residents that the state was taking their property by eminent domain for a public beach and recreation area. They were given no options.

"Relocate or your homes would be demolished," Herter told a gathering of residents at a meeting at the former dance hall on Gooseberry Neck. It was easy for him to make that pronouncement as he did not seek re-election, but was appointed Secretary of State by President Eisenhower a year later. If most residents had not been forced out, it is believed most would still be there today or at least until Hurricane Bob arrived in 1991.

So the moves began. Five homes were transported by Jim White, professional house mover, up Main Road to Cornell Road into Adamsville, Rhode Island. Trees were trimmed and lines were moved as houses passed up Old Harbor Road and down Howland Road to their new ocean view - but not oceanfront - resting places. Other beach homes were moved north on Horsencek Road miles up-river and reestablished on Shirley Street on the East Branch. Some other homes went to Small's Village, a development next to the Bayside Restaurant near Second and Third Avenues. Other cottages from a conclave on West Beach called Cooper's Cottages were moved to Drift Road.

Although Carol negatively impacted many Westport residents, this was not the case for Steve Howland who sold the bulk of his lots after the hurricane. The first house on the east side of Hillside Road was Ray Smith who drove us to the club. Below Smith, there was Ray Davis' little cottage. Ray Davis was born in the Davis farmhouse before it was converted into the Acoaxet clubhouse and well after the British launched a cannon ball into the original structure.

To the south of Davis was the water supply for Steve Howland's properties and high above the dug well was a water tower, which was blown over and now on its side. The water tower was a holding tank for drinking water and it was one of many in Westport Harbor, (including one on the then-fourth-hole of the golf course which some golfers tried to hit to ricochet the ball onto the green.) Other water towers and windmills were situated in the Acoaxet area or along River Road on the east side of the Harbor to provide water to that specific area. Next to the water company was a three-stall garage for farm equipment and storage of other items that were needed by farmer Howland. Across the road from the water works lot was the Smith's porch overhang that nearly killed us all only hours earlier.

Next was our house, its red roof proudly still intact despite the absence of selected shingles covering its ranch design. To the south of us was a vacant lot that Howland hoped to sell as part of his approved subdivision plan for what is still called the lower Howland Road area. All the remaining lots were empty along Hillside Road except for Smith who had bought a double-lot to live next door to the west of his brother, Cliff, on Lakeside Avenue.

When Carol arrived in 1954, Betty Mills Coolidge and her husband Frank took their three very young children 100 yards up Lakeside Avenue to higher ground to safety at her sister, Louise Mills Borden's home where they rode out the storm. The Coolidge family home unlike the Mills home on the beach during '38 was located away from the ocean but was still within the flood zone from rising pond water during Carol.

To the south of us was the Whitin house. To the east of us and about six feet lower and at sea level were two structures owned by Mrs. Avis Sturtevant - her main house and a cottage called the "Dog House." Mrs. S had lived there since 1926 and remained until 1961. The high water flooded the "Dog House," as teenager Hank Truslow found when he swam to rescue the elderly lady. Truslow discovered the water had reached the top of her doorway but fortunately she had evacuated. Her main house where Dr. King resided as a tenant was on cinder block pilings. Some pilings moved and the house tilted to the north after the storm but never collapsed.

The high water mark reached our property line on Whitin's land and Sturtevant's lot but never reached us. This supported the prediction by Steve Howland earlier in the day that we would be fine if we stayed right where we were. The old farmer was right. Our house took in some water from leaks due to the intensity of the wind-driven rain, but fortunately no flying debris came through the large east-facing picture windows nor did the tidal surge enter our property as film taken by Mr. Rodgers can attest. Take that for precise weather forecasting, Al Roker!

From our house to the south though was near-total devastation. We walked the area in silence and with disbelief. None of our neighbors spoke. Everyone just stared. Nature had temporarily broken the human spirit.

At the southeast and southwest corners of Howland Road and Atlantic Avenue were two sets of bathhouses - each had approximately 50 individual lockers plus shower stalls and rest rooms. As Howland Road continues to the ocean, the Foster family owned the cabanas to the right. Mildred Foster was the daughter of George W. Howland, a brother of Steve Howland. The Foster bathhouses and snack bar was sent sailing up Richmond Pond along the shoreline over a quarter mile to the north. They slid past the Foster home, which had taken on water in the lower level and required Mildred and her son, Howland, to climb out the rear window to the north. By exiting in that direction they were protected from the wind. They scurried through the fields to the safety of the Hindley house, which had become a rallying point for those living in low-lying areas.

The Foster house had at one time been the corncrib on the site of the larger Howland farmhouse on the west side of Howland Road. Howland sold the large farmhouse and two-level cow barn prior to hurricane Carol. The Howland family then moved the corncrib down the road to the intersection of Howland Road, Atlantic Avenue and Richmond Pond Drive where it sits today after multiple additions.

It was during that time that Mildred Foster assisted Steve in running the hotel (he summoned her to come back from Connecticut because all "Howlands belong in Westport," reported Howie Foster). She lived in the three-story, 16-bedroom hotel with one full bath, one half-bath and two water closets with her son and was joined by her husband, Stuart, on weekends.

The Fosters bathhouses and snack bar was not the first facility of its kind at that location. Prior to the '38 hurricane the Howland family had owned and operated a beachfront sit-down restaurant very much like Plante's pavilion on Horseneck Beach. The facility was not a snack bar but a full-blown restaurant on the beach. The "Long Island Express" wiped it out in 1938. It was replaced further inland on the property by a 32 unit bathhouse facility set on wood pilings along with a small snack bar for patrons. There were showers and rest room facilities and a small addition was made to add more lockers before Carol came to town. After Carol, the Foster bathhouses that had been moved were cut up and returned back to their original site away from the ocean by means of a road cut through the fields. A smaller snack bar was added and was operational for another six years until the 1960 hurricane, Donna, the fifth major hurricane in 22 years to hit the southern New England coast with winds exceeding 135 miles per hour. After that the Fosters decided to call the food business quits. The bathhouses were eventually sold but are still standing today and owned by CK Beach Club.

The bathhouses on the left side of the road that extends all the way to the waterfront, known as the Howland Pavilion, were originally set aside for use by the guests of the Howland Hotel. Built in 1894, the Pavilion was destroyed in 1938 but after being rebuilt, it fared better in subsequent storms probably due to the large rocks in front of them on the beach. The rocks were attributed in part to Mother Nature and in part to the creativity of Steve Howland.

As Howland was cutting roads into his fields to develop his house lots, he needed to dispose of the soil and rock that was excavated from Hillside Road, Pierce Road and Russell Road, now called Fairway Drive. Much of the rock was ledge and was blasted free and trucked away but not far. Some could not be moved, such as the large rock that still sits today at the south end of Hillside Road and drivers must by–pass it. Miraculously, to this date, no motorist has ever lost the battle with the large rock. The most likely accident victim would be the person who has had the greatest number of opportunities to navigate around the rock, and that is your author.

Howland directed the excavation and road crew to take the ledge and rock down the road and dump it on his beach between the ocean and his bathhouses and two rental homes. After all, it was his property, he could do with it what he wanted even if it was on the beach, couldn't he? This would never be allowed today.

Eventually, it came to serve as an important barrier from the effects of ocean storms.

To the east of Howland Pavilion still stands a small one-bedroom cottage and to the east of that there is still a four-bedroom house on the beach, owned today by Howland Beach Properties. Howland Foster is a principal owner of that enterprise and is the great-nephew of Steve Howland, and his only heir. The houses, too, were spared in the hurricane due in part to the wall of rocks and ledge.

Renters, Mr. and Mrs. Warren and Mrs. Read occupied the four - bedroom cottage at the time. They were neighbors in Pawtucket, Rhode Island, and invited young Axel Larson to spend summers with them in Westport Harbor. Mr. Read had died in the cottage of a massive heart attack a few years before Carol despite the quick action of young Axel and the prompt response of next-door-neighbor, Doctor Antonio (Tony) D'Angelo. Mrs. Read returned the following year with the Warrens and the child that neither couple ever had - Axel. Fortuitously, on August 31, 1954, Axel's parents had taken him on an end-of-summer trip to Maine. Mr. Warren had gone to work and the two ladies remained alone in the beachfront rental. It was not until the waves crashed over the front lawn into the rear yard that Mrs. Warren decided to leave. Joined by her friend they drove out of the property just in time. They were heading to Pawtucket but less than a mile from the shore on Old Harbor Road, they were prevented from further travel by a downed tree in the middle of the road. They did an about- face and joined the gathering at the Acoaxet Club where the crowd was growing by the minute.

Both rental homes did survive but not without damage. The front and rear stairs on the home occupied by Warren, Read and Axel were sent packing along with the glass-enclosed sunroom on the southwest side of the cottage. The stairs were replaced but the sunroom was not.

Next door and closer to the ocean was a cabana owned by two ladies named Eastwood who also owned a more substantial house on the west side of Howland Road only two houses north from the corner of Atlantic Avenue. The Eastwood ladies would arrive at the cabana at 10 a.m. daily, enjoy a swim and some sun time before driving back up the road to prepare and have lunch. They would return at

2 p.m. for another two-hour stint before making the short trek up the road in time for tea. According to Axel Larson, this happened daily all summer until Hurricane Carol demolished the cedar-shingled cabana for the final time.

The houses on the beach to the east suffered the same fate as the Eastwood cabana. There was a remnant of a chimney and concrete walkway from the Shaw family cottage. Nancy Shaw May remembers reconvening after the storm had subsided at the Hindley house where her father had arrived from Connecticut after driving through the storm to reach his family.

"He told us that he and a group of other desperate motorists had worked together to remove a fallen tree from a road along his route. He also described his feeling of shock when he finally rounded a corner on Howland Road and saw the beach-empty of houses except for the shells of Rhee and D'Angelo homes. Of course, at that point, he didn't know what had happened to his family. It must have been an awful feeling," Nancy recalled.

The good news was that everyone in the Shaw family survived. Blitz was finally off her leash and running free again albeit amidst the ruins, and Miz Ma'amselle was found in her cage on the kitchen table, wet and unhappy in the flooded, but intact, Eddy house.

The Shaw family lost their cottage, which was also a prefabricated design like Richardson's, to the pond. The Richardson's cottage washed across the street and landed in the middle of Atlantic Avenue. The Shaws eventually rebuilt after buying a lot from Steve Howland across from Ray Davis on Hillside Road, the same lot where the Smith roof landed nearly killing us on the morning of the hurricane. The Shaw house in the pond collapsed when it hit the rocks in front of the Mills home on Lakeside Drive and was later disassembled and trucked off the shoreline and stored in pieces in Steve Howland's garage next to our home awaiting reconstruction on their new lot two years later. The Shaw family vacationed in that small three- bedroom cottage on that site into the 21st century.

Next door to the Shaw house on the beach was the 1950 beach house of Dr. Tony D'Angelo and his wife, Blanche. Tony loved three things: Blanche, cigars and golf - not necessarily in that order. His short, shirtless frame could be seen nightly practicing his golf swing in his Atlantic Avenue front yard with an ever-present cigar hanging from the corner of his mouth. His golf clubs in the heavy leather bag complete with a pint of bourbon for medicinal purposes only was always stored in the trunk of his car in case of emergency. The day Carol arrived Tony was seeing patients in his office in nearby Bristol, Rhode Island, so his car and clubs were safe.

But Blanche and her car were not. The auto was in the garage at the beach house and not only did Blanche's pink Caddy end up in the Cockeast Pond across Atlantic Avenue, but all of her jewelry was also AWOL. She had walked to the Hindley house and then hitched a ride to the Acoaxet Club but all her personal effects remained in the house. The house was a shell; furniture and appliances were all over the sand-filled front lawn. Her family photos as well as her clothes were also missing. Blanche enrolled neighborhood kids to help search for her jewelry. Kids were all more than willing to lend a hand, since Mrs. D, as she was called, was always exceptionally kind to all the neighborhood kids, providing us with ice cream treats from her freezer every time we cut through her driveway going to or from the beach. The ice cream guy in the truck equipped with the calliope music and bell to attract attention must have hated her. She cut right into his profits.

The Caddy in the pond to right, author's home is upper left. (Photo courtesy of Lorna Phan and Holly Bronhard from the Dr. Tony D'Angelo collection)

It was not just the kids that lent a hand. Neighbors came from the safety of their homes on the hill to assist beachfront residents who had been hardest hit. People began cleaning the streets, vacant lots and front yards of those who welcomed the comfort and support. In a time of crisis, people come forward to assist others, forgetting their own needs. There was the sharing that Americans are known for: people helping people.

To the east of D'Angelo's was the Rhee house. The water had rushed in the front door and out through the rear, across Atlantic Avenue into Cockeast Pond and up onto the Acoaxet Club property. The water took with it furniture and fixtures as it did with all the beach homes. Personal possessions along with household items and children's playthings including bicycles with rubber handlebar grips with vinyl streamers and bells or bugle horns were found buried in the sand and rubble from the force of the storm.

Dail Rhee had arrived in the U.S. in 1951 to live with his aunt Vonnie and uncle Dan, cousin Mike, and grandmother Maria Chung, in the beach house that Dan and Vonnie had owned since 1946. In the off-season they all lived near Newport, but this house like most homes in the Acoaxet area was a summer place.

"On the morning of the Hurricane day, Aunt was on a trip and Uncle Dan dropped me off at Mr. Borden Tripp's well known country store in Little Compton (Adamsville). I had a summer job at the store and usually I would be heading home on the bus in the afternoon. However, on that day, Uncle Dan and cousin, Mike, came back to the store to pick me up after the storm news was broadcast. We came back to Acoaxet via upper road, the Acoaxet Country Club road, to look for my grandmother (Uncle Dan's mother), who was in the house. She was 80 years old and did not speak any English," related Dail, who now lives in Hawaii and never returned to Westport after the year of the storm.

To the east of the two- story beachfront home of the Rhees were two homes that took unscheduled rides up the Cockeast Pond. Mrs. Alice Potter, widow of Wallace, owned one, while Henry Otte owned the other. Their homes also came to rest in the pond along the banks of the Acoaxet Club. Local handyman Wib Smith moved the Potter house to the east side of the pond and rebuilt it on his land on River Road where it remained until 2007 when it was torn down. The two houses that were unceremoniously moved off the beach were later replaced with cabanas used primarily for day visits to the beach. The Potter and Otte families owned lots of land on Howland Road that they purchased (from Steve Howland, who else?) near the Howland

The remains of the Rhee home near Beach Rock in the Harbor. (Photo courtesy of Lorna Phan and Holly Bronhard from the Dr. Tony D'Angelo collection)

Hotel in 1959 and 1955 respectively. They eventually built homes on those sites. The cabanas remained in front of Beach Rock for years until Bob, a cousin of Carol, showed up in 1991. One of the cabanas is still in use near the dock at Cockeast Pond as a storage facility for pond boat accessories.

Next came the foundation of the Gallery home. As much as the Fall River surgeon loved his golf and Balantine Ale, he would have sacrificed both to have his house still on the beach rather than in the pond on the shore of the golf course. It had been swept from the southeast to the northwest by the blowing wind and surging sea. His wife, Charlotte, was in the home during the early part of the storm but escaped in time to be part of the group at the Acoaxet Club. Fortunately, she could not see through the large salt-covered windows of the Acoaxet Club dining room to see her home, tilted sideways in the pond on the distant fairway below. The terrifying ordeal seemed to change Mrs. Gallery who never again seem to be the same. After that experience she and her husband did, however, buy two Steve Howland lots in March 1955 in the lower Howland Road area and built a new home in a much safer location on high ground.

As we progressed along the beach to the east, we were prevented from moving farther by a six-foot-wide by three- foot-deep gulley of raging water that had breached the road. It streamed from south to north between the ocean and pond. The water at the newly created inlet was retreating back to the ocean but was still flowing rapidly in the late afternoon. It had cut through the sand and rocks like a knife through butter. The sand and the asphalt were gone; Mother Nature had temporarily created a new river. The green sea grass and rosa rugosa had been covered by brown foam from the churned-up ocean. Atlantic Avenue looked as if it had been chewed up and spit out. Sand and seaweed replaced asphalt and walking along what once had been a road or even the beach was now a major undertaking. Rocks, the size of small boulders, littered the landscape. Carol, as she rushed from the ocean, unearthed years of accumulated sand that had provided a comfortable resting place for beach rocks. Walking along this former sandy beach and asphalt road was now a hazardous undertaking.

To the east and in the distance we could see the remnants of the Elephant Rock Beach Club. Only a section of the structure and the pilings was still there, most was to the north in the parking lot or in Cockeast Pond. We also soon discovered that a slice of River Road at the herring run had also washed away.

The section of Westport Harbor known as Acoaxet including the Boathouse Row area was isolated. No phones, no electricity, no water, no sanitary facilities but significantly less damage than the west side of the Harbor, which was also without utilities: no electricity therefore, no light, no water and therefore, no plumbing. Day-to-day conveniences that are taken for granted had come to a halt. The absence of electricity was not unique to Westport and lasted for two weeks for some, while other sections of town were restored in a week after Carol hit. The loss of the "life blood of the modern community had ceased to flow over the wires," reported the Providence Journal in its hurricane summary booklet. The lack of electricity also prevented 25-cent per-gallon gasoline from being pumped and cars from moving. It took Yankee ingenuity to solve the problem. Locals hooked up belts from their lawn mowers onto gas pumps thereby allowing gasoline to be pumped into waiting cars, trucks, tractors, boats and lawn mowers.

After we crossed the newly created inlet, we continued our mission to the east across what was Atlantic Avenue. We were trying to determine if our friends, the McDuff family, who were renting a home at the corner of Atlantic Avenue and Acoaxet Road, were safe.

When we reached the Harwood home that the McDuff family had rented, things had changed indeed. Before the storm hit, the cottage had run east to west with an outside breezeway connection between the bedrooms and the living space. Now, the cottage bedrooms were facing south to north and the connection was missing after the hurricane. The force of the water had moved the house around and had hijacked the personal possessions of Mrs. McDuff as it went through the structure.

After the phone call from my father earlier that morning, the family had taken things seriously and began to vacate. The warnings of their young daughter had gone unheeded until the phone rang.

Chassie tried to wake her parents as the rain came onto the bed in their room, but her parents were not budging. Fortunately, they also had a live- in babysitter for the week in the person of Sarah Bullock Desjardins whose parents lived four miles north in Adamsvillle. Off to Adamsville in mid-morning they drove, but first Mrs. McDuff needed to gather and bag the family sterling silver flatware, which she had brought from their residence in Providence. Not only was the silver expensive but a family heirloom with great sentimental value.

They jumped into the car, drove up River Road and passed the ill-fated bus heading in the opposite direction. Little did they know at that time that their rental home would be on an island for days to come after the ocean surged over Beach Avenue and Atlantic Avenue and the river broke through the herring run.

The family did return to the house the next day. Mrs. McDuff in her haste to leave had left her sterling silver monogrammed hair-brush, comb and mirror in the bedroom. The search for the items of sentimental and real value took the family into the sand, which had covered the yard. After sifting through the sand and debris for hours, the personal items were found. But the McDuff family never returned to vacation in Westport Harbor again.

Nothing moved in or out of Acoaxet for days - not even the mail from the post office despite the slogan of the U.S. Mail: "Not even rain nor snow can stop the mail from being delivered on its appointed route."

But Carol did!

CHAPTER 17

Rock and Ruin

Almost every house in the white sandy dunes of Horseneck and West Beach was destroyed. They were privately owned beach properties that were taken by eminent domain by the state after the storm. East Beach and Gooseberry Neck, a 73 acre peninsular that extended from the beach areas out into the ocean, were also destroyed. Eighty-five percent of all the homes in this area were either destroyed or left like splintered wood on the beaches. In fact, of the 200 cottages built on beach areas in town between 1949 and 1954 only 20 remained. Some were then transported to lots owned by Steve Howland in the lower Howland Road neighborhood of Westport Harbor, while others were relocated to an area off East Beach called Smalls Village. Another group ended farther up off Horseneck Road on riverside lots. There were less than 20 homes on the expanse of beach in Acoaxet. Of the homes or structures that stood in the early morning of August 31, 1954, most were either destroyed or nearly gutted. A few were rebuilt and remain today but the sea generally completed another cleansing of her shore in 1954. The majority of oceanfront homes had been destroyed in 1938 and most owners had learned their lesson: Don't mess with Mother Nature.

"Statistics generally fall flat," according to Polk Lafoon in his book Tornado, the story of the tornados to hit Xenia, Ohio, in 1974. "People are impressed, briefly, when they learn that an outbreak was unusual, but then they recall that natural disasters of one sort or another occur with modest regularity and their attention wanders," said Lafoon.

And so it was in Westport in 1954. Those who witnessed the events of the day and lived through those events recall them as vividly as the day President John F. Kennedy was shot or the World Trade Center was attacked on September 11, 2001. While images become cloudy with time, it is remarkable how many who experienced that day can retell their own stories over a half-century later.

Natural disaster survival is a tribute to the human spirit. The facts are often blurred by time but the gist is the same: it was a disaster of monumental proportions that none would ever want to experience again. In fact, some never spoke of it again, such as teenage bus occupants, Dana and Mary. The experience they shared would warrant discussion but it was not to be. Mary was a college girl and Dana a high school boy at the time. Both nodded and said "hi" as they passed each other on the football field in Swansea, Massachusetts following the annual Thanksgiving Day rivalry game between Case High School and Somerset High School. Dana was a Case team member and Mary's brother played at Somerset. That was it. They never saw each other again.

Each year on the Saturday of Labor Day weekend, a dinner/dance at the Acoaxet Club is held to bid the summer farewell. But on Labor Day weekend in 1954 the festivities were canceled due to the severity of the behavior of one uninvited female. No band, no buffet dinner, no drinking from members' bottles brought into the clubhouse for set-ups, no late night of carousing and one unanticipated night of peaceful sleep for a non-dancing neighbor to the north. A tropical disturbance, named Carol, was the spoilsport to the end of summer.

The final round of the Charlton Cup would be played on the first Monday in September 1954. That tradition would continue, the golf and tennis matches would be played and Phinney would see to that! Nothing would deter Phinney who was later awarded a $250 bonus by the Board for the extra work he had done to prepare the facility for the club's members to complete in the golf and tennis championships over Labor Day weekend. Everett V.D. Mills, the club president and brother of Betty, "Wee Anne" (who nearly drowned in GH38) and Louise Mills Borden, presented the trophies on Labor Day and the tradition continued.

The Red Cross established a Relief Station at the Westport Town Hall after Carol and started a Disaster Fund Campaign to raise money to aid hurricane victims. Five thousand dollars was paid out in the first week but there were no disaster stations in either the Harbor/Acoaxet or the Point/Horseneck areas where the most destruction occurred. The essence of effective disaster relief - getting aid delivered to victims in the form of whatever is needed as quickly as possible in a matter of minutes or hours at worst - was not met on the coast. It seems as if that objective is rarely met as those who have been touched by Hurricane Katrina and the earthquakes in Haiti and Chile in 2010 can attest.

The town of Westport was faced with the reality of the clean-up situation. Selectmen J. Douglas Borden, John A. Smith and Norman Kirby approved a "sum of $20,000 as an Overdraft on Hurricane Damage" according to the minutes of the selectmen's meeting of September 13, 1954. A week later they signed regular warrants and specific warrants for hurricanes Carol and Edna. Carol cost the town $15,897.79 while Edna added an additional $12,440 in unbudgeted expenses. The total represented 3.3% of the total town expenditures for that fiscal year, as was reported in the town annual report. The majority of funds were paid in overtime costs to town employees in the police, fire, tree and highway departments-people like Fred Cambra on 24-hour bulldozer shifts.

Reserve police officer Dana Reed was twenty-eight years old at the time, and married to Zola. They had three sons under age eight, the youngest a two–month-old baby. On the day the hurricane struck he had car-pooled with a friend to their jobs in Providence at manufacturer Browne and Sharp. When they concluded their shift, Dana's friend's car was under water in the street. Dana began his odyssey back to Westport. He was able to hitch a ride to the State Police barracks in Dartmouth and after a call to Westport Police Chief, Charles Dean, a car was sent for Reed. It was the beginning of 130 straight hours of police duty for the reservist. He did not see his wife or family for the next five days.

Reed was given a Jeep pick-up with four-wheel drive courtesy of Davis Chevrolet, a new car dealership in town on Main Road. Chief Dean then sent Reed on his way to the Horseneck area of town. It would take a four-wheel drive vehicle, not the 1937 Indian Scout motorcycle that Dana generally drove, to maneuver the washed out areas. Reed crossed the Point Bridge and headed for Plante's Pavilion. Driving along sand-covered roads, he would often catch a phone wire on the bumper of the Jeep and it would snap like elastic as the vehicle moved along. He headed up to the Midway Restaurant on 16th Avenue and then to the causeway at Gooseberry. The four-wheel drive on his vehicle allowed him to pass over the chewed-up terrain and find three survivors in the tower, the eighty-four–year-old Reed related in 2009.

Upon his return to headquarters in Central Village he was given another assignment. Looting had become prevalent and he and Charlie Lees joined fellow auxiliary officer, Bill Pierce, who had his shotgun with him as they headed out on river patrol. They stayed on land and in the water for the next four days protecting the valuables that many homeowners believed they had lost in the storm.

Westport farmers like Steve Howland and Borden Tripp were also negatively impacted by the heavy wind damage that destroyed corn crops, especially silage corn that was used to feed their livestock. The sagging corn stalks, now coated with salt, signaled the premature end of the growing season.

Noquochoke Orchards, the one-hundred-acre apple and fruit and dairy farm, experienced destruction to its buildings and half its trees. The gale winds took down the silo and the roof off the barn that was home to 30 cows, as well as the roof of the house. Peaches, plums and premature apples littered the fields and ruined the orchard's prospects for the fall. Located two miles inland south of the Head of Westport on Drift Road and six miles north of the ocean on the west bank of the east branch of the river, the farm has been owned by the Smith family since 1899.

On the day of the storm sixteen–year-old Caroline Smith, next to the youngest of five children, was scheduled to work at her summer job as a soda jerk on the beach at the Spindrift. Her mother, a single parent at the time due to the untimely death of her husband, refused to drive Caroline down to the oceanfront business at ten o'clock in the morning since the storm was in full force. That may have saved the teenager's life.

All the children went to school and worked on the farm in addition to summer jobs to help their mother financially. The sale of the fruit and milk was crucial to the family since, at that time, there was no such thing as welfare. Working on a farm was hard work and it often was an incentive to children to finish their education. Caroline, in fact, went on to study at Bryant College on scholarship after graduating from Westport High School.

The orchard/farm has survived multiple hurricanes over its 110-year history but this was the first time the family saw a restaurant sitting out in the river near their shoreline.

By the end of the day, the miles of Westport oceanfront shoreline looked as if it had been shelled. There was no power or phone service and that was common throughout New England. The salt spray stripped the land of the smells of autumn, and the aroma of the wild red grapes was missing in 1954. The lack of utilities caused Mary Tripp Wicks - the Ma in Bojuma Farm - to leave town with her two daughters, Judy, 11, and newborn, Liz, and head back to their winter home in Pennsylvania. They had ridden out the hurricane in their cottage on River Road over a mile away from the ocean. They could observe the activity on the river from their picture window that Judy was not permitted near for fear it would implode. They witnessed the boats tear from their moorings and boathouses explode off their pilings and rush up-river on automatic pilot. Only days after returning home to Pennsylvania, they were forced to move again due to the massive inland flooding caused by Hurricane Edna.

By the time Dail Rhee and his cousin Mike reached the Eddy house on Atlantic Avenue late in the afternoon after the storm had passed by, they were within a 100 yards of their home. The sun was shining and the air clear, but when Dail and his cousin stepped in and looked around, debris and sand were everywhere. The front half of the lower floor of the house was gone. Shards of windowpane glass protruded from the sand in what was the ocean-facing living room. The remaining furniture was soaked and the water stains had crept up the partitions. Dirty, wet clothes littered the floors, chests were overturned and pictures that once hung on the walls littered the sand-covered floors. The water was four feet deep at that point in time but they reached their house only to find that their grandmother was missing. They later discovered that friend Dick Shaw had saved her life.

The Rhee family left Westport and drove to their year -round home, returning the next day to assess the damage and search for the family dog. As the Rhee cousins searched the battered house, they called for their dog: Here, Wou - Wou! Here, girl! Come, Wou - Wou!

From under a bed on the second floor came the cold, wet and shaken collie who had survived one of the most destructive hurricanes ever to reach the New England shores. Rhee recalled: "The following morning, when we returned to look for the dog, the water had retreated and the house was still standing; although the ground floor was wiped out and only the posts were holding up the second floor. We found our collie on the second floor."

Rhee and Shaw never had contact with each other from that day as the Shaw house was destroyed and Rhee never returned to Westport despite spending four years at Massachusetts Institute of Technology only 65 miles away.

Less than a year later the 80–year-old Maria Chung returned to Seoul, Korea. She never returned to America.

For Westport kids it was time to explore. But it was a dangerous time. Boards and shingles with rusted nails littered the landscape. Enormous snapping turtles, which had lived in Cockeast Pond, began their slow march out of the now brackish water over the golf course to safety and a new refuge. The size of these dangerous reptiles can be 8 to 18 inches long on average with large heads that do not retreat into their shell and use their bite for protection. While they are vicious on land, they generally shy away from swimmers in the water and retreat. They had been disturbed and they were upset, it was time to stay away as they made their trek to a new home.

Items were strewn all over the Harbor from the beach to the pond to the parking lots to the grounds of the Acoaxet Club and neighboring shorelines. Furniture and clothing littered golf course grounds. Twelve–year-old Nina Truslow joined some of the older children as they sorted through items of interest. Nina found some neat Indian madras shorts that fit her. She headed off only to be intercepted by Louise Mills Borden, who lived in a home just off the eighth green and who reprimanded Nina for taking something that did not belong to her.

"Nina, you are looting, you cannot take that," said Louise, according to Anne Tripp Hopkins who was one of the older kids (age 15) in the excursion party. A find that was even a bigger hit with the teens that day, which they did not return, was a refrigerator full of cold Ballentine Ale. MM!

One of the items discovered by twelve–year-old Borden Snow, who went exploring the flotsam on the golf course was a small non-descript five-drawer chest. The boy's salvage instincts took over. Upon opening the draws Snow discovered treasure.

"One drawer was full of heavy monogrammed sterling silver," said Borden. "I found an empty golf bag and filled it with knives, folks and spoons. I determined it belonged to the Rhee family and delivered it to Dail," recalled Snow. The golf bag also belonged to Danny Rhee.

On his travels, Snow found a telescope used primarily for bird watching and stargazing. "I was into that stuff, viewing the stars when I was a kid. I took the telescope home, took it apart, cleaned it up and repaired it for use," said Borden. One day he had the telescope in his front yard pointing out into space when a car, traveling along Atlantic Avenue, stopped suddenly. The driver wanted to know where Borden had gotten the telescope. Borden explained his find and the driver said; "Hey kid, that's my telescope that went up the pond with my house in the hurricane. I want to have it back," said the obviously impatient and still distraught resident. Borden said fine, and right then and there returned it to Dr. Gallery. For years afterwards items were being recovered from Cockeast Pond.

As recently as March 2010, members of the Acoaxet Club grounds crew unearthed an item in the light grass rough near the banks of the pond on the eighth hole. The blackened piece of metal seemed to rise out of the land. After being cleaned and polished, it was determined to be a small four-inch-long by three-inch-wide piece of sterling silver. It was engraved with unfamiliar initials but may have been a portion of a lady's hairbrush. Without doubt, it was a remnant of either Carol or GH38. In either case, there are undoubtedly more artifacts from those great hurricanes waiting to be resurrected.

Refrig and other debris adorn the fairway at the Acoaxet Club.
(Photo courtesy of Anne Tripp Hopkins)

The water that came rushing through the herring run in Westport Harbor to the north of the Harbor Inn/Ogden's after the storm was like looking at the Nile River, according to Borden Snow. To the south of the store on Atlantic Avenue, the ocean had sliced through the asphalt roadway. The rush of river and ocean water into Cockeast Pond brought with it guests that did not fare well, according to Rick Borden, who was 12 at the time. Rick reported salt-water fish were catapulted into the pond, "Big stripers, probably 30-40 pounds. When I was 12 they looked 60-80 lbs. They died because the water was brackish and not salt and most froze in the ice later that winter." Rick lived with his parents, Rick Senior and Louise Mills Borden, in a house on high ground next to the eighth green and ninth tee on the Acoaxet Club. His grandparents - the Mills - lived next door and hosted the Otte house on their property during the storm. Their Coolidge cousins from down the lane and twenty-eight-year-old Aunt Betty, who nearly drowned in the 1938 hurricane, joined him, and his younger brothers that day in their house. All witnessed the bathhouses smash into Gull Rock and the series of beachfront homes wash past their picture window onto the shores of the pond.

It may have been as long as three weeks before power was restored to Westport Harbor. Many homes cooked and heated water with propane gas. Without electricity to pump water many of the residents were forced to leave their summer homes. Not the Borden's.

Since they were located adjacent to the Acoaxet Club property and the club had its own gas generator for power - the Club had water. As a result, Ed Phinney ran a line from the club over to the Borden's house - smart man that Phinney, as Rick Borden, Senior was the long time treasurer of the Club and signed Phinney's paychecks. With water and gas for cooking, the Borden house became the most popular spot in the Harbor. Families would come to the house to cook meals and the Borden's neighborliness was rewarded with many a cooked meal left behind.

"We never ate better," said Rick Jr.

Unlike Horseneck Beach, which could be reached from Horseneck Road, and Westport Point that was at the end of Main Road, the Acoaxet section of Westport Harbor was an island. For the Branch family there was a silver lining to the storm. Since their house was now uninhabitable - water had reached three quarters of the way up the first floor walls - sand and seaweed covered the floors and fish were swimming in their living room. Everything in the basement was destroyed. The Charlton family decided to relocate the house to higher ground on River Road across the road from Ogden's Store. But, in the meantime, the Branch family was provided interim housing in the mansion as they waited for renovations to be completed for more permanent housing. Wayne remembers that he initially was allocated one of the servants' rooms but for some reason was moved into "the second floor bedroom called the 'Oriental Room,' which was a huge bedroom with a giant bath, ornate tapestries on the divider, a lavish embroidered spread on my four poster bed and I did my algebra homework on a gilded table/desk with a masterful view of the Atlantic," he related.

For a few days after the hurricane, the view from the "Oriental Room" included gold fish splashing in the ocean water in the front yard of Pond Meadow. Carol had displaced them from the confines of their enclosed pond along Beach Road.

One of the hurricane's few benefits occurred at Oggies. Due to the lack of electrical power to keep items frozen, kids, even adults, lined up for free melting ice cream products. The free ice cream became the store's loss leader. Dick Colby recalls asking Miriam Ogden why the prices on other store items had doubled. "She tersely told me: 'We've had a hurricane,'" recalled Colby. And an inquiry to plumber Everett Coggeshall about when might the water system be repaired, sparked a similar disinterested response: "summer is over. You people can all go home." The skukes were getting a clear message.

While the National Guard patrolled the roads in Westport, the looters were out in force in Westport Point. On the night of the hurricane, a new $600 boat was stolen from the yard of Mrs. Albert Scothes on Main Road. The Herald News reported that Fred Manchester and Josh Robbins, both of Westport, were later apprehended for the theft. They were not the only ones trying to take advantage of the disaster.

According to printed newspaper reports, Manuel Alfredo from a section of Westport called Petty Heights, his twenty-six–year-old son from Fall River and two other unidentified Fall Riverites escaped the vigilance of Dana Reed and shot-gun-toting Officer Pierce, but they were still arrested for looting the Westport Lobster Pound in Westport Point.

Less than forty-eight hours after the Yacht Club water festival ended, the clubhouse, its sixty bathing lockers, the docks and all the boats were attacked by the tropical cyclone of breathtaking proportions. And whatever was left suffered a second blow as Edna followed Carol two weeks later and finished off whatever her cousin had left behind. Commodore Kelley, who succeeded DeNadal, now had the unenviable task of navigating the membership through a reconstruction project.

The members of the family club where children learned to swim and sail and even water ski were devastated but vowed to rebuild. Many were Westport residents, some even watched from their homes on the Point as the water engulfed their club.

The camaraderie at the Yacht Cub was such that volunteerism flourished. The nearly 200 family members would come together and rebuild, repair and be ready for the following summer season. Most of the small boats were gone and the lockers had been taken off their wood pilings and relocated on the property but they were salvageable. So was the main clubhouse. It took a barge brought down from Fall River by club member and construction company owner, Godfrey "Buck" Bassette, to reposition the lockers and the main building on new concrete pilings. Only a matter of feet separated the new locations from the old. Before the hurricanes, the lockers were located on the west side of the clubhouse and they ran north to south. Their position after the hurricane was to the south/east of where the main building had been placed. The demand for lockers was such that this presented the perfect opportunity for members to construct and attach another section of 30 lockers to the original design.

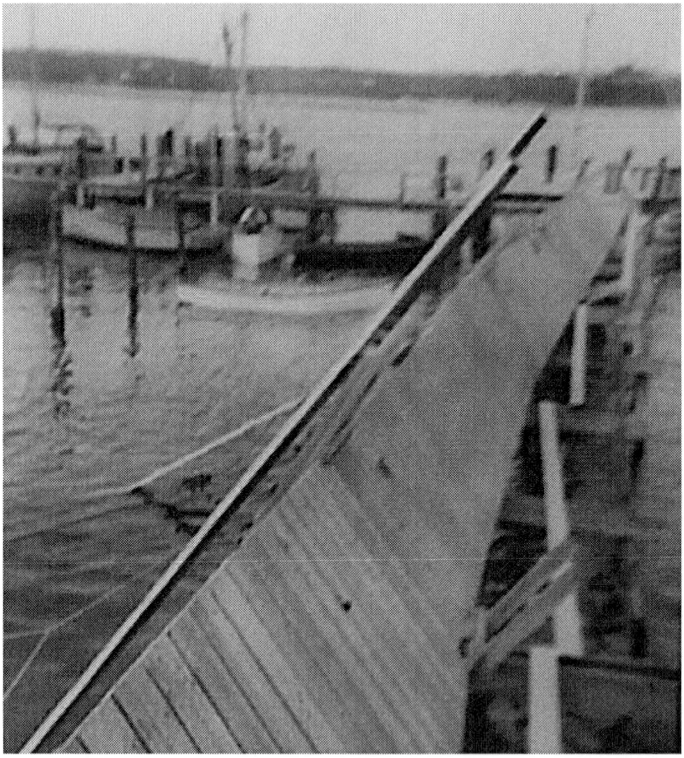

Yacht Club dock up ended.
(Photo courtesy of the Westport Yacht Club)

CHAPTER 18

The Survivors

Cozy Cab bus after being submerged.
(Photo courtesy of Lorna Phan and Holly Bronhard from the Dr. Tony D'Angelo collection)

Cozy Cab bus service to and from Westport Harbor ceased a few years after Carol. Jimmy could be spotted driving a taxi in Fall River for the family business far from the dangers of the sea. Periodically, however, he would substitute for the regular beach route driver and some recalled how nervous and even shaken he was years later when traveling along the oceanfront Atlantic Avenue. Seventeen years later, he died as a young man at age forty-seven leaving behind a wife and two children. He left behind a son in the Navy and a daughter who was living in Westport and working at the telephone company in Fall River. A delegation from the Cozy Cab Bus Company attended his funeral service.

Mary McGowan went off to college and eventually became a teacher. She married, had a family and still resides in Somerset, the same town where her parents lived when she went off that day to catch the bus from Fall River to Westport.

Dana Plante went back to Case High School in Swansea and then went on to Wesleyan University in Connecticut, graduating in 1959. He joined the military and died from a viral infection while undergoing training.

Dale Plante spent most of his adult life in Rhode Island, as a landscape architect and town planner. He maintained an office, coincidently enough, on Howland Road in East Greenwich. He is retired and living in Arizona.

The storm was so bad on Nantucket, according to Charles Orloff: "even the Coast Guard Rescue Boat was unable to hold its mooring." Orloff noted that the most dangerous threat resulting from a landfalling southern New England hurricane is storm surge, which is a result of wind pushing water toward the shore. The continental shelf and the shallow slope of New England's coast can exacerbate it. "The threat is compounded by the shape of Narragansett and Buzzard's Bay," noted Orloff.

In 1954, Carol was the costliest United States hurricane to that date with over $460 million in damages. Westport alone suffered at a price tag estimated between $800,000 and $1,000,000 and along the beachfronts of the town there was nothing left but sand. It is estimated by some that even to this date, Carol was the most damaging hurricane in Massachusetts history and more damaging to southeastern Massachusetts than the Great Hurricane of 1938. Nearly a half billion dollars in damages occurred in the Northeast with hundreds of boats and yachts as well as homes and businesses destroyed. It would take Congress 16 more years to pass a national disaster plan. The multiple natural disasters of the 1960's - Hurricanes Carla, Betsy, and Camille as well as the Alaskan Earthquake - caused the federal government to develop a comprehensive strategy to assist those impacted since the Red Cross could no longer meet the financial demands of victims from the voluntary generosity of the general public. Federal compensation to individuals and businesses for natural disasters was fragmented at best until then. In fact, in 1960, the government had no ongoing natural disaster assistance plan. In 1970, a Disaster Relief Plan was passed by Congress and amended to increase public support two years later. But it was costing the government a small fortune. A year later the reimbursement levels were eliminated entirely and interest rates for loans spiked.

What had not been totally beaten up by Carol felt the effects of Edna less than two weeks later. Edna took the same Atlantic path as Carol but passed over Martha's Vineyard and then the outer limits of Cape Cod. Because the most dangerous part of a hurricane is the right quadrant, Edna did not prove to be particularly destructive to Westport - certainly not like her cousin, Carol. She added fuel to a still smoldering fire, however, and helped finish the job started by her relative. Her rainfall was five to eight inches and combined with Carol's five to seven inches, streams and rivers again ran over their banks and produced widespread flooding. Since hurricanes are named alphabetically and at the time were recorded as females, one was missing between Carol and her cousin, Edna, only 12 days later. She was Dolly; a fast moving tropical wave that became a tropical depression on August 31 while Carol was smashing into the southern New England coastline. Dolly became a tropical storm later that day, and a hurricane on September 1st. After reaching a peak of 95 miles per hour winds, Dolly became extra tropical within two days. The hurricane season of 1954 had one more punch left. On October 15th, Hurricane Hazel brushed the area with light winds and rain. Some termed her a "sissy."

Three more storms of note landed in Westport over the next nearly 40 years: Donna, Gloria and Bob. There have been other major hurricanes to hit the New England coast. Less than a year later in mid-August 1955 Diane made her way to southern New England, weakening to a tropical storm and dropping heavy rainfall on the area which caused major flooding and millions more in property damage. After a five-year hiatus, Donna arrived in 1960 with wind speeds in excess of 100 miles per hour and heavy pockets of rain. Donna made land fall in Westport on September 13, 1960, and became the ninth costliest hurricane in U.S. history at that time. By the time she reached the shores of Westport, she had lost much of the punch that had been felt from the Carolinas through New York. The winds were strong as was noted by the Blue Hill Observatory near Boston and recorded at over 145 miles per hour, but the storm was accompanied by little rainfall. And while she did not cause significant local damage, she was the only hurricane to affect every state along the East Coast with hurricane-force winds.

It was twenty-five years later before another major hurricane threatened Westport. On September 27, 1985, Gloria slammed into the Connecticut shore with Category 3 winds. Despite being on the right quadrant of the storm, Westport was spared the effects of the strongest recorded hurricane to strike the East Coast so far north. It is a distinction she still holds today. By the time she departed she had been downgraded in the seasonal post analysis.

What happened in 1938 and 1954 should not be repeated.

Hurricane Bob, unlike his two immediate predecessors, made a real mess of Westport and brought a premature end to the summer of 1991. Residents of the southcoast of Massachusetts had plenty of warning for this cyclone. Television had tracked him up the coast with the expert eyes of the National Hurricane Center providing updates.

On August 19, 1991, Bob made landfall in Newport, Rhode Island, placing Westport on the most dangerous right quadrant only a few miles away. He arrived with winds topping 100 miles per hour as a Category 2 storm. The wind reached speed of more than 125 miles per hour and touched off tornados in both Rhode Island and Massachusetts. He caused a storm surge of over 10 feet and the area between Newport and Cape Cod was the hardest hit. Two areas in nearby Mattapoisett lost 61 of the 72 homes located in one section of the town. Westport residents lost power, trees and waterfront homes, while beaches lost up to 50 feet due to erosion. Boats again were destroyed but at Tripp's Boat Yard, they had learned from Carol and were better equipped to handle the storm. They were able to remove over 200 boats from the water to the safety of their storage facilities. Rain was not a factor in the storm as less than an inch fell in Westport. But Dr. Tony D'Angelo's house on Atlantic Avenue in Westport Harbor was again gutted. The doctor and new wife, Mary (Blanche had died), vowed to rebuild. And rebuild they did.

The salt stripped the trees of their leaves and left summer residents with a sense of total loss. Thankfully, there were no victims. The golf and tennis tournaments continued at Acoaxet and sailing and swimming classes went forward at the Yacht Club with much less enthusiasm. This was a new generation, which, by and large, had not experienced a hurricane except on television. Bob brought them a new realization and respect for the power of Mother Nature.

A storm does not have to be categorized as a hurricane to do coastal damage in Westport. Over the years since Carol and then Bob, multiple Nor'easters, as they are termed, descend on Westport and bring incredibly large surf, high winds and heavy rain or snow. The remaining beachfront homes on Horseneck and Westport Harbor are buttoned up and have been free of serious damage. East Beach is another story. Rocks from the now abbreviated beachfront cover East Beach Road, frequently requiring the town bulldozers to clear a passage to John Reed Road. There are no longer many permanent or substantial structures on that beach and what summertime homes remain (mostly trailers) are towed from the site and taken inland by their owners. Except a few brave deep sea-fishing trawlers tied up at the docks at the Point, boats have generally been lifted out of the river and are in dry dock for the winter. Hence, little to no boat destruction occurs.

But waves still crash and water still creates beach erosion and breaches Atlantic Avenue in Acoaxet as recently as December 3, 2009. Winds blew steady at around 25 miles per hour with gusts to 60. Nearly two inches of rain fell and the full moon tide-like Carol's-caused the water to rise to unusually high levels that morning. Ghosts of hurricanes past were further uncovered by eroding sand. The missing steps of Doctor French's beachfront pre–'38 home protruded from their sandy grave only to be nearly submerged again a few months later. The foundation from the Ruth Charlton and Fritz Mitchell home in front of Pond Meadow protruded more from the sand again. The remains of the Gallery's pink concrete foundation

2009 Winter Nor'easter overtaking Beach Rock.
(Photo courtesy of Paula F. Cummings)

base rose even higher to remind observers of past natural disasters and what the future may hold.

The number of hurricanes to reach the New England area from 1938 to 1960 is six. In the past 55 years there have been an equal number. Hurricanes are fed by warm water and the northern Atlantic waters are warming. The next logical step in global warming would seem that more hurricanes should be arriving in New England. The results of the past nearly 55 years in comparison to the prior 20 would seem simplistically and unscientifically to demonstrate that the waters are no warmer or there would be many more hurricanes reaching Westport. But perhaps not.

A study released in early 2010 predicts that global warming will influence the number of storms and the damage those storms would create. The report suggests that hurricanes with winds more than 130 miles per hour would nearly double by the end of the century. It concluded that there would be fewer but more powerful storms in the Atlantic basin, according to research meteorologists at NOAA.

The World Meteorological Organization decides which storm names will be retired due to the severity of their impact. Edna, Diane, Donna, Gloria and Bob have all been retired and will not be used again. Nor will Andrew and Katrina, two of the largest hurricanes to make landfall in North America in Florida and Louisiana.

No area will ever again be impacted by a cyclone named Carol.
She too, has been retired.

In the 1960's scientists developed what they thought was a solution to halting the movement of a storm into land. The concept was to tow an iceberg from the Arctic into the warm southern waters of the Atlantic and deposit it to melt in the path of a cyclone. It would then cool the waters and take away the source of strength from the hurricane thus diminishing its destructive force before landfall. It didn't work.

Billionaire Microsoft founder Bill Gates and a team of scientists tried another theory in 2009 to reduce the deadly and costly affects of hurricanes before they destroy us. Hopefully, their theories will prove more successful than the iceberg theory of nearly a half-century ago. But just in case:

Be Prepared

“When descends on the Atlantic
The gigantic
Storm-wind of the equinox,
Landward in his wrath he scourges
The toiling surges,
Laden with seaweed from the rocks.
Ever drifting, drifting, drifting
On the shifting
Currents of the reaches
Of sandy beaches,
All have found repose again.”

“ Seaweed”
H.W. LONGFELLOW

Acknowledgements

This account of the fury of Hurricane Carol in 1954 would never have taken its final form if it were not for Mary McGowan O'Toole. Mary's first hand account of her harrowing voyage aboard the Cozy Cab bus inspired the author to refocus and direct this story telling to the events that occurred on and around August 31, 1954.

Special thanks also go to Dale Plante who recalled the events of that day for himself and his brother, Dana, with great accuracy, as did Nancy Shaw May and her brother, Dick. They provided detailed recollections.

Locating Dail Rhee in Hawaii also turned out to be fortuitous since he collaborated the story of the Shaw family among others, and provided teenage memories of a day from hell for the South Korean family.

Tom Rodgers, Bordie Snow, Janet Rattray, Paul and Wayne Branch, Charlotte Brayton Underwood, Suze Brayton, Eileen Sheehan, Anne Tripp Hopkins, Sonny Carter, Wendy Hanson Baker and the Wicks sisters-Judy and Liz-were kind enough to retreat into their memory banks and find interesting and in some cases, life saving bits of information from that day.

Albert E. Lees III opened up the family photo and postcard library to me while Fred Cambra and Dana Reed provided first hand accounts, as did Dick Colby and Madeline Hamel.

Ralph Cross opened the doors and history of the Westport Yacht Club and Lois Souza McCormick recounted her untold story of the activity on Horseneck with her family. Lynn and Sue Carter related being in the middle of the action at the Point. Thanks to Holly Sirois, Lorna Phan, Holly Bronhard and Ursula and Bennett Brown who provided photos of the storm's destructive powers.

The most emotional story came from Stephen Bigoness who I tracked down in Connecticut. His mother, Paola is still living but did not want to relive that day when her child was swept out of her arms forever. Stephen was kind enough to relay the details of the family tragedy.

Many others allowed their stories to be told: Sarah Bullock Desjardins, Charlotte and Henry McDuff, Tony Perini and Lee Pelton Morrison, Howland Foster, Hank Truslow and Jim Whitin; Sheila DeNadal Salvo, Axel Larson,

Susan Phinney Ashworth, Frank Coolidge, Jr., Brenda Figuerido and Caroline Langlois, along with Rick Sisson, Jane Welsh, Charlie Cowing, King Cruger and Richie Earle. Jenny O'Neill and Anna Duphiney at the Westport Historical Society and author, Pam Carey were also very helpful.

A thank you to others who may have not realized that they had been helpful to this effort: Harry Powers, David Cummings, Al Gaudet, Ray Helger, Oscar Sylvia, Doug Amaral, Mike Elephante, Jim and Author Liz Waring, Martha Manchester, Dr. "Chip" Garnett, Judith Hindley Guider, Marge Sandborg, Charlie Messier, Steve Carney, and Joan Agler at the International Tennis Hall of Fame, the staffs of the Westport Assessors Office and Selectmen Office, Mary Faria from The Herald News, Steve Hurley from the Massachusetts Department of Fisheries and Game.

There are those whose accounts appeared in local news media or in video recordings who should also be recognized: Paul DeNadal, Bill Tripp, J. Roger Sisson, Roger Reed, George Yeomans and Bill Hart.

Special thanks to my long-time friends whose advice I value greatly: David McIlwaine my former co-worker and especially, Warren G. Hathaway, Publisher Emeritus of Hathaway Publishing Corp. for his words of praise.

To Mary Senra and Laura Paquette at Senco Printing, Inc. for their excellent suggestions and Atty. Deborah Basile for her legal advice as well as my internet guru, Mary Lou Kroll of POWW Media Services.

A debt of gratitude is also owed to my new, good friend Carlton "Cukie" Macomber. A life-long Westport historian, Cukie's observations of the events surrounding Hurricane Carol and his comments about the book that appear in the Foreword are deeply appreciated.

To my former English teacher at Portsmouth Priory School, Reverend Dom Damian Kearney, O.S.B. a special thank you for taking the time to review the manuscript and offer suggestions prior to publication and, and to my editor, Tracey Minkin who gave me the encouragement I needed to complete the task.

To best selling author Ann Hood, -thanks for her kind words.

To my wife Paula who was my sounding board, I/T consultant and business manager, this could not have been published without her.

Published Sources

A Look at Westport Through Four Centuries 1976 - Westport Bicentennial Commission

A Wind To Shake The World-The Story of the 1938 Hurricane - Everett S. Allen-1976-Little, Brown and Company

Carol at 50 :Remembering Her Fury: A Historical and Pictorial History of Hurricane Carol - Charles T.Orloff- Blue Hill Observatory- 2008

The Herald News - September 1954 Editions

Hurricane 1954 - The Standard Times, New Bedford

Hurricane - New Bedford Standard Times September 1944

Images of America Westport - Westport Historical Society-Arcadia publishing -2008

Lincoln Park Remembered - Spinner Publications 1999

Sudden Sea - The Great Hurricane of 1938 - R.A.Scotti-2003 – Back Bay Books-Little, Brown and Company

The Charlton Story: Earle Perry Charlton 1863-1930 - Earle P. "Chuck" Charlton II and John Hoey, April 19, 2006

The Complete Historical Record of New England's Stricken Area September 21, 1938 – Hurricane - New Bedford Standard Times

The Fabulous Fifties as Recorded in The Herald News - Historical Briefs, Inc. 1991

The Great Hurricane 1938 - Cherie Burns-2005-Grove Press

Tornado - Polk Laffoon-New York: Harper and Row- 1975

Westport's Deadliest Storm Reliving the Hurricane of '38 - The Traveler-The Journey of the Westport Historical Society

Westport Enters its Fifth Century - Westport Historical Society-2001

Westport Shorelines - 2004

Westport Experiences : A Dark Side of Nature –The Hurricane of 1938

Westport Point Bridge - Carmen Maiocco-1992

Internet

Hurricane Carol
National Weather Service
NOAA
Wikipedia

Videos

50th Anniversary Reunion at The Paquachuck Inn
Beverly Schuch, Interviewer
Mike Cushing… Cameraperson

Published Papers

A Prospectus of Goosewing Beach in West Acoaxet, Massachusetts and Little Compton, Rhode Island, R.I. - Philomena E. Truesdale, M.D. 1934

Hurricanes Into Hop - John W. Cummings 11, Esq.—1956

Hurricanes in New England 1635-1996 - Sarah Bishop Valentine

Hurricane Westport Harbor - Richard K. Hawes, Esq.-1938

University of Arizona-Hurricane Research - Professor Elizabeth Richie-March 2010

History of Coxet, and the Richmond Family - Henry Worth

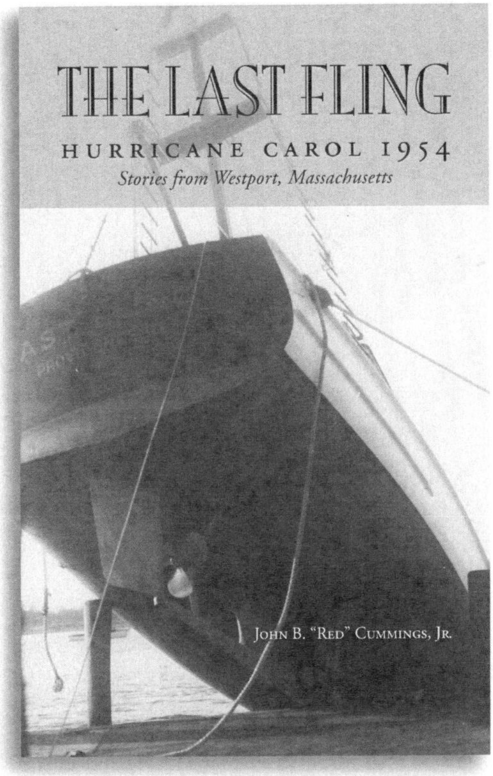

For additional copies of

"The Last Fling"

please mail your orders to:

The Last Fling
46 Hillside Road
Westport, MA 02790

By Phone:
50.636.2831

Visit us on the web at:
www.thelasrfling.net

ISBN 978-1-4507-7648-6

ORDER FORM

PLEASE PRINT

Name ______________________________

Addresss ______________________________

City______________________________

State/Zip______________________________

Email ______________________________

___ @ $24.95 per copy______________

___ add 6.25% sales tax (MA Res. only)

___ Add $3.95 per copy shipping and Handling

___ **TOTAL**

PLEASE DO NOT SEND CASH

Enclosed is my check for $ __________

Please charge $ ______________ to my
☐ VISA ☐ MASTERCARD ☐ AMEX
Card # __________________________

CVV ______(3 or 4 digit verification # on card)
Exp. ____________________________

Signature ________________________